Praise for Rabbi Mel G
And God Created Hope

"Rabbi Glazer's book is filled with kindness, compassion and insight into every kind of loss in the human experience. He tells us the stories we love and shows us how to wander through the desert of loss, find faith, strength, and joy, even in our sorrow. This is a book well worth reading for all of us who grieve."

—Kathleen O'Hara, MA, author of *A Grief Like No Other:*
Surviving the Violent Death of Someone You Love

"Grieving the loss of a loved one is like being in a different country without a map. We lose our bearings. *And God Created Hope* helps us transcend our lostness while also helping us reconcile death as a part of life. The scripture references and personal stories that Rabbi Glazer weaves throughout the book provide reassuring directions as we wander through our grief. Though the specific journey differs for each person, it is through hope that we eventually heal. And this book helps us find hope."

—Mary Polce-Lynch, PhD, author of *Nothing Left Unsaid:*
Creating a Healing Legacy with Final Words and Letters

"[Grief] is an age-old problem so it is quite appropriate to go back to the Bible and learn from our predecessors about how to deal with the loss of loved ones, be they pets or family, and express our grief. I truly think reading this book will help everyone because thinking about the subject and your personal experience is what needs to be consciously dealt with. The memories live on within us and need to be acknowledged and experienced and the wounds healed."

—Bernie Siegel, MD, *New York Times* best-selling author of
Love, Medicine and Miracles and *101 Exercises for the Soul*

Rabbi Mel Glazer, DD, DMIN, *received his Doctor of Divinity degree from the Jewish Theological Seminary and his Doctor of Ministry degree from Princeton Theological Seminary. A congregational rabbi for more than thirty years, Rabbi Glazer is a prominent grief recovery specialist certified by the Grief Recovery Institute. He trained directly under John W. James and Russell Friedman, authors of the definitive work* The Grief Recovery Handbook: The Action Program for Moving beyond Death, Divorce, and Other Losses *(New York: HarperPerennial, 1998). Rabbi Glazer has counseled, lectured, and conducted workshops in the interfaith community across the United States and Canada and has contributed articles and chapters to theological and general interest publications and books. His work has been featured on TV, radio, and the Internet, and he writes a column, "Your Grief Matters," for the* Pocono Record *(Pennsylvania). Rabbi Glazer lives with his wife, Ellen, in Stroudsburg, Pennsylvania.*

And

God Created

Hope

Finding Your Way
through Grief
with Lessons from
Early Biblical
Stories

RABBI MEL GLAZER

Foreword by Russell Friedman

Marlowe & Company

New York

Library of Congress Cataloging-in-Publication Data

Glazer, Mel.
  Finding your way through grief with lessons from early biblical stories /
Mel Glazer ; foreword by Russell Friedman.
     p. cm.
  ISBN-13: 978-1-56924-267-4 (trade pbk.)
  ISBN-10: 1-56924-267-4 (trade pbk.)
  1. Consolation (Judaism) 2. Hope--Religious aspects--Judaism. 3.
Grief--Religious aspects--Judaism. 4. Bereavement--Religious
aspects--Judaism. 5. Death--Religious aspects--Judaism. I. Title.
BM729.C6G53 2007
296.7--dc22
            2006035823

This book is dedicated to
Rabbi Kenny Berger, of blessed memory…my friend,
and Rabbi Harry H. Epstein, of blessed memory…my Rabbi.

Yea, though I walk through the valley
of the shadow of death, I will fear no evil,
for Thou art with me...
—Psalm 23:4

Hope is the thing with feathers that perches in the soul,
and sings the tune without the words, and never stops at
all.
—Emily Dickinson

Nothing can bring you peace but yourself.
—Ralph Waldo Emerson

Once you choose hope, anything's possible.
—Christopher Reeve

The risk of love is loss, and the price of loss is grief
But the pain of grief
Is only a shadow
When compared with the pain.
Of never risking love.
—Hilary Stanton Zunim

Contents

Foreword
by Russell Friedman

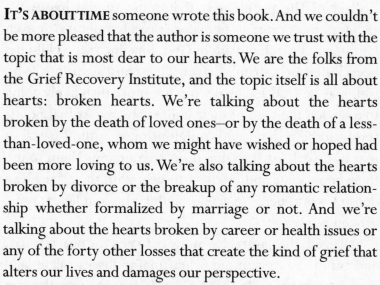

IT'S ABOUT TIME someone wrote this book. And we couldn't be more pleased that the author is someone we trust with the topic that is most dear to our hearts. We are the folks from the Grief Recovery Institute, and the topic itself is all about hearts: broken hearts. We're talking about the hearts broken by the death of loved ones—or by the death of a less-than-loved-one, whom we might have wished or hoped had been more loving to us. We're also talking about the hearts broken by divorce or the breakup of any romantic relationship whether formalized by marriage or not. And we're talking about the hearts broken by career or health issues or any of the forty other losses that create the kind of grief that alters our lives and damages our perspective.

At their respective cores, Judaism and Christianity share a most profound piece of language: "And thou shalt love the Lord thy God with all thy heart, and with all thy soul, and with all thy might." The word "heart" is enhanced to point out that it is the first of the three elements included in this passage. I mention that because after twenty years of helping people deal with death, divorce, and a host of other major losses, there's something I can tell you without fear of contradiction. When the emotional heart is broken, the spirit or soul cannot always soar; and when the heart is broken, the might of the intellect often does not work. Lest you think I am being critical of people's religious or spiritual beliefs, let me assure you that is not the case. I am reporting what more than twenty-five thousand grieving people have shared with us at the Grief Recovery Institute over many years.

Part of the problem is that some of the losses we encounter can cause us to experience a temporary, or even long-term, breech of faith in God. Imagine that a child has been killed by a drunk driver. That child's parents, who well may be God-loving people, are more than likely going to question the God of their understanding. At that point, trying to help them with religious or scriptural passages may not work. At the same time, encouraging them to use their knowledge and intellect to deal with their grief also doesn't work, because grief is about a broken heart, not a broken head.

All in all, the natural harmony between the heart, spirit, and mind is interrupted when major losses occur and disrupt our lives. *And God Created Hope* bridges the gap between the heart and those scriptures that can effectively address the emotional impact caused by death, divorce, and other losses. Rabbi Glazer's personal relationship to profound losses, coupled with his religious learning and grief recovery training, make him the perfect messenger to help get the heart, spirit, and mind back into harmony. When we are able to address our broken hearts with the correct tools, our hearts, souls, and minds can soar again. That idea can give you the hope to read this book and find the tools and actions contained within it that can help you better your life and the lives of others.

For many people, hope is buried under a lifetime of habits, many of which were developed in response to losses or the incorrect information we learn about dealing with loss. As we practice what we learn, we develop a kind of emotional muscle memory that causes us to repeat actions that do not benefit us, and it becomes harder and harder to either recognize the underlying habit or to change our knee-jerk reactions to people and events. A major element of the difficulty of change is the familiarity of the habits we've perfected over the years. We will often defend to the death our right to be wrong about the mistakes we repeat over and over. And as we repeat these unhelpful actions, we lose hope that we will ever get it right.

Spiritual, religious, and psychological programs that promote change share a common denominator: that there must be new and different actions to get new and better results. The same is true for physical health, whether related to food and diets or to alcohol or other substance abuse. Without new habits to replace the old ones, change is not possible. Habits are nothing more than memorized actions. This book, like all successful programs for change, is based on action.

When people see or hear the phrase "grief recovery," it's often the first time they became aware that recovery from significant emotional loss is even possible. It is my wish that you will take hope from that idea and then apply that hope to the ideas and actions in this very special book, *And God Created Hope.*

From my heart to yours, with love and most of all, hope, Russell Friedman.

Russell Friedman is executive director of the Grief Recovery Institute Educational Foundation (http://grief.net) and coauthor of The Grief Recovery Handbook, When Children Grieve, *and* Moving On.

And

God Created

Hope

Part One

LAY THEM GENTLY DOWN

Introduction

〜

And God Created Hope for Me, Too

I HELP PEOPLE say good-bye. I help them stop carrying their deceased loved ones around in their heads, grieving. I have the gift of walking through the valley of the shadow of death. Not many people are comfortable with that, but I am. Perhaps it is because death visited my house very early on.

My father died in 1959, just two days before my twelfth birthday. I did not get to say good-bye, and I was not allowed to go to the funeral. Neither were my younger brother and sister. As a result, I could not even say the word *Daddy* for thirty years. The problem is not really that he died, it is that, for me, he never lived. He worked all the time and I hardly knew him.

I was born and raised in Atlanta, Georgia. My mother, Rose, was born in Atlanta, but her parents were born in Russia. I really could not tell you what she was like, because, although I know she loved me, she never let any of us get close to her. We did not have a good relationship and, as I learned later, neither did my parents.

My father, Abe, was born in Poland and came to the United States just after the turn of the century. He owned a grocery store on what is now third base of Atlanta's Fulton County Stadium. I never saw him much. He left before I got up in the morning and he came back after I went to sleep. He was home only on Sundays. I have just two memories of him: on Sundays he used to make us pancakes, and although he never went to the synagogue otherwise, on the High Holy Days—Rosh Hashanah and Yom Kippur—he was there from the beginning to the end, and I would sit with him and snuggle under his big tallis, the Jewish prayer shawl.

My father was never affectionate, and he had a violent temper. The last year of his life, he was not working—he was at home, sick. But neither he nor my mother told me or my brother and sister what was going on. The day he went to the hospital for the last time, I hid in the bathroom when the ambulance came to get him. I was afraid of seeing him on a stretcher or seeing him go to the hospital. I was afraid, because I did not know what was happening. Not only did my mother never explain anything to us, she gave us the clear impression that we were not allowed to ask her about it, either.

We're still not sure what happened, but as best as we can figure out, his appendix burst, and during surgery the doctor may have clipped an artery. My father bled to death.

He was only forty-seven. After he died, my mother still never talked about it and never spoke about him again.

My rabbi became my father figure, and I was the son he never had. He saw something in me and nurtured that intellectual spark. Much to my surprise, he offered to put me through school. First he raised the money to send me to Philadelphia to Akiba Hebrew Academy for my high school education, then to New York for college, where I went to Columbia University in a joint program with the Jewish Theological Seminary. There were no strings attached. He did not do any of this on the condition that I become a rabbi, and he made that very clear to everyone, including me. His name was Rabbi Harry H. Epstein, and he led the Ahavath Achim congregation in Atlanta for a remarkable fifty-seven years. We always remained close.

In the late 1990s, when Rabbi Epstein was about ninety-five, I took my son Ilan, who was in college at the time, to see him. "One of the most important things I ever did in my life was to teach your father," Rabbi Epstein said to my son. We were all overcome by the power of those words.

I knew that I might never see Rabbi Epstein again, so I asked to talk with him alone. "We do not hide anything from each other," I said to him when we were alone. "And I know that we may not see each other again. So I want to thank you for everything you've done for me and everything you've been to me." We both cried.

Only recently did I realize that with that visit I had the opportunity to do with him what I hadn't been given the opportunity to do with my father: I said good-bye.

As it turned out, that was not our final good-bye. In the spring of 2003, I went to Atlanta to celebrate Rabbi Epstein's one-hundredth birthday at a party given for him by friends. He came to the party in a wheelchair, but was able to enjoy himself.

About a month later, in May, the synagogue threw a huge birthday party for him, but he was not well enough to attend. So they videotaped the party and brought the tape to him at home later that night. He watched the tape and then, peacefully, he died.

For many years, I have been intrigued by the Old Testament's lessons about grief and the hope that can follow. Yet very little has been written for laypeople about this subject. Such wisdom should be shared beyond the confines of clergy and scholars, shared with people of all denominations (and none at all) who need consolation, understanding, and hope. Humans have always told stories, listened to stories, read stories, and acted out stories in an effort to understand themselves, their world, and the other people in it.

The themes of early Bible stories—not only those that have been chosen for inclusion here that teach us about grief—are just as useful in understanding the human condition today as they were thousands of years ago when they were first told. Throughout this book, with the help of the wisdom of these Bible stories, I hope to teach you how we can complete our relationships with loved ones and with others who have died, how to "lay them gently down," and how we can tackle grief's key issues so that we may move beyond grief—not merely dwell in it and cope with it—and into a life of hope and fulfillment. In other words, "to go from mourning to morning."

This book is not an analysis of particular Bible events. Rather, *And God Created Hope* uses these stories as a jumping-off point to learn from the themes they represent on the path through grief recovery.

When We Can't Lay Them Gently Down

Death is never a welcome visitor. As much as we'd like to wish it away, it comes, relentless and uninvited. And death never seems to come at just the right time. Sometimes it comes too early, sometimes too late. Is there ever a right time for death's visit?

Sometimes death is not an enemy. Death can bring a merciful end to a life that has been racked by pain or physical or mental incapacity. But even then we are left with heavy hearts and troubled souls. We loved those we lost so much that we want to keep them close to us, in our hearts forever. Saying good-bye is so difficult for us, letting them go is so painful. And sometimes it is easier if we just let them stay with us and hold on to them for dear life. We want them to be part of our lives in the future just as they were in the past. How can we possibly go on without them, without our love for them and their love for us? With them, we had life. Without them, we feel empty inside.

But must we feel so empty? Is clinging to our loved ones always such a good idea? Won't clinging to them slow down our continuing growth as men and women who deserve love, passion, and contentment?

It is the way of the world for people to die and for us to live on (and love on) after they've gone. We have a hard time saying good-bye to our loved ones who have died, and because of this, we often have a hard time getting on with our lives. Many of us know people whose loved ones died more than a decade ago, but who still have problems today grieving and moving on. Nothing has changed for them since that sad day when death came to visit. It is as if their loved ones are still there, living and breathing. In these situations, the living can't let go and move on. They're stuck. And as long as they can't get unstuck, the dead for whom they grieve are still alive, while the grievers who still live and breathe are deadened to life, unable to live fully.

Something is wrong here, upside down, and the grievers know it and feel it. The dead are alive, and the living are dead. This is not what was supposed to happen. The dead were supposed to die, and the living were supposed to adjust to their new lives. What we hope for is life with vitality, but what we too often get is continuing pain and broken hearts. It's as simple as this: if the dead aren't allowed to die, the living won't be allowed to live. But as hard as it is to let go, that is precisely what we must do.

We are most challenged when we have to give back something that was dear to us. Our world teaches us well how to acquire things, but not how to return them. We're like children who do not want to share—our toys, our possessions, our loved ones. We want to keep them with us forever, but we can't.

It is okay to still miss the people we've lost. Missing and grieving are two very different emotions, and throughout our journey, we will learn to tell them apart.

My goal in this book is to teach you how to "lay them gently down," that is, how to allow your dear ones to part from you with love so that you can then proceed through the stages of grief and come out the other side to experience hope and joy. It is not always an easy task, but I assure you it is possible.

We rabbis like to share a Zen story now and then, and the one I am about to tell has become one of my favorites. It helps us understand how often, and in how many diverse ways, we can carry around with us what we should let go.

Two monks set out on a long journey. After a while, they came to the shore of a river, where they saw a beautiful young woman who needed to get to the other side. One of the monks picked her up and carried her through the deep water to the other side of the river, then he put her down on the shore. He said good-bye, and the two monks continued on their way.

Twenty minutes later, the second monk chastised the first, "Brother, you did a terrible thing back there. You know we are not supposed to touch a woman."

The first monk turned peacefully to his friend and said, "Brother, I put her down twenty minutes ago. Why are you still carrying her?"

That seems to be our problem, as well. We continue to carry those who have left us. We miss them so much that we do not want to put them down. We continue to carry them around with us, hoping that somehow that means they're still alive. But, alas, that is not the case. They have died, but we've not yet truly said good-bye to them.

They are dead, yet still alive. We are still physically alive, yet spiritually dead. Something is terribly wrong when we live like this, and we feel it every single day of our lives.

Learning through Loss

Throughout my years of studying, teaching, lecturing, writing, and counseling in the areas of dying, death, and the grieving process, not only as a rabbi, but in the interfaith community and as a certified grief recovery specialist, I have come to this one startlingly simple conclusion that I call Glazer's First and Only Law of Life: *We only learn anything about ourselves by how we respond to the losses in our lives.* We only realize what we had when we do not have it anymore. Grief, therefore, can be a dynamic opportunity to learn and to grow.

Throughout our loss-related learning experiences, we always ask: *How do we recover from our losses? Not forget them, but recover from them?* The answer lies in how we respond to loss. Are we beaten by it, or do we grow from it and learn to transcend it?

Every person grieves differently. And one person can grieve different losses differently, depending upon an almost infinite number of variables that stem from a few basic circumstances: what they lost, whom they lost, and how the loss occurred. ·

The loss of relationship is what we really cry about. We mourn not just the past, but also a future that will no longer include the person we mourn.

Let the healing begin.

Each chapter of this book begins with an early biblical story that illustrates that chapter's theme. In part 1 we will look at core grief topics that help you understand loss and healing:

- bargaining and prayer (Jonah)
- death is part of life (Ecclesiastes)
- tragedy (Lamentations)

In part 2 we will look at the common themes that people encounter on their healing journey through grief:

- shock and anger (Leviticus)
- ritual (II Chronicles)
- fear (Exodus)
- wandering and healing (Numbers)
- faith and strength (Job)
- forgiveness (Genesis)

These are presented in the order we typically experience them, though of course we can also deal with these themes not only out of order but simultaneously as well. Nothing about the grieving and healing process is written in stone.

In part 3 we move "from mourning to morning" on our grief recovery path:

- grief without death (Song of Songs/Solomon)
- joy (Proverbs)
- growth and wisdom (Psalms)
- legacy (Deuteronomy)
- the future: creating new relationships and creating a new family (Ruth)

And in the epilogue we reflect on a surprising twist we often encounter even when we think we've got everything all figured out.

Although experts have documented the process with official stages of grief, everyone who grieves knows that how we grieve is often just a free-for-all. Taking all of this into account, we can safely say that there are only four major steps in the grieving process, as ridiculously simple as they may appear:

- grief
- coping with grief
- false grief recovery actions (When we think we've let go, but we haven't.)
- letting go of grief

How do you know you've completed this four-step process, that you are okay? You will know when you've created a "new normal," when life is no longer upside down, when you no longer feel that the dead are alive and you are dead. You will know when you finally let go and lay your loved ones gently down, knowing that God created everything. And God created hope.

CHAPTER 1

Bargaining and Prayer

The Story: Jonah and the Big Fish, from the Book of Jonah

⁓

OFTEN WHEN SOMEONE we love takes ill and death becomes a real possibility, we pray to God to ask him to let our loved one live, to heal him or her, so that life can continue as it has in the past. And sometimes we will make bargains with God. It happens often, and as you will soon read, it happened first in the Bible, thousands of years ago.

Jonah was a prophet, but we do not know very much about him. Well, except for his legendary run-in with a really big fish. The story begins when God commanded Jonah to go preach in the city of Nineveh that unless everyone there repented their sins, they and their entire city would be destroyed.

Instead, Jonah boarded a ship headed for the town of Tarshish. During the voyage, a severe storm arose that threatened to destroy the ship and everyone on it. The sailors thought if they sacrificed someone to their gods, the storm would stop. They cast lots to determine whom to sacrifice, and the lot fell upon Jonah. Jonah told them about his God and how he had disobeyed God, so the sailors prayed to Jonah's God not to use this storm to punish them for Jonah's sins. Then they threw him overboard.

Immediately, the storm subsided. The sailors believed this was the power of Jonah's God. "Then the men feared the Lord exceedingly; and they offered a sacrifice unto the Lord and made vows."

Once overboard, God promptly arranged for a really big fish (not a whale, as has been incorrectly translated) to swallow Jonah. For three days and nights Jonah was trapped in the fish's belly, miraculously undigested, praying to God to get him out. Jonah prayed, he bargained, and finally God spoke to the fish, which then followed his command and spit Jonah out upon the shore.

Once again, God commanded Jonah to go to Nineveh. This time, Jonah went. He told the people of Nineveh that if they did not repent their sins, God would destroy them and their city within forty days. The people and their king repented: they fasted, wore sackcloth, and did not even drink water, hoping that God would spare them. It worked. God was pleased that they had repented and had turned from their sinful ways, and he did not destroy them.

Prayer Is Bargaining

When we pray, we're actually bargaining with God. We ask for something and promise something in return. Even when we do not propose a trade, we're still engaged in a form of bargaining, even though it appears to be just begging. In these cases, we're trading our belief in God's powers for God's help.

When we grieve, we're often at the height of our bargaining and praying. Even people who never pray otherwise find themselves bargaining with God or simply just begging for help when a loved one has left, is sick or dying, or has passed on. Even though none of us gets out of here alive, and we've all gotta go sometime, we pray for the dying to be spared. We often pray even harder when the dying aren't elderly, when we feel that they're being taken from us "before their time."

In the story of Jonah, we see three clear instances of bargaining: the sailors offer a sacrifice, praying that in exchange the storm will subside; Jonah prays to be spit out of the fish's belly in exchange for obedience to God; and the people of Nineveh repent in exchange for God sparing their lives.

When we bargain with God, we believe that if he listens, he'll either give us what we ask for or turn us down. If we do not believe God is listening, what we really mean is that he is there but not paying any attention to us. If he listens, and gives us what we want, we believe our prayer has been answered, and the answer is yes. But what if the answer is no? What if a loved one's leaving, or death, leads us to believe that God turned down our prayer request? Unfortunately, we often believe we've been turned down because we're not deserving, or, in the case of death, because our loved one was not deserving. So now, not only are we grieving, but we're feeling guilty, frustrated, ashamed, and perhaps even misunderstood. Now we're in pain and feeling about two inches tall.

Bargaining implies some form of a relationship with God, but it is a phony relationship. It doesn't work, because it is a conditional relationship, not an unconditional relationship. The word "if" makes the relationship conditional: "God, if you _____, then I'll _____." How often have we heard ourselves, or others, say a prayer that goes something like this: "God, if you spare Grandma, then I'll come to [insert your house of worship] more often." Is God thinking, "Why don't you just come more often anyway?"

What does God think of us when we pray and bargain? Does God act like the parent of a kid who's away at college and say, "Why do you only turn to me when you want something? Why don't you want to have a full relationship with me whether you need something or not?"

If you believe in an all-powerful God, bargaining will make sense to you, because you think that God can do everything and that you can influence God to change his mind, be charitable, or compassionate. And if you do not have a day-to-day, unconditional relationship with this all-powerful God, you are even more likely to believe that he will give you what you want.

If you do have a day-to-day, unconditional relationship with this all-powerful God, you are actually less likely to believe that he will give you what you want, so you are less likely to bargain. Why? Because you do not view God as simply a part-time errand boy. The faithful, so to speak, believe they do not have to bargain, because they believe

God already knows what's going on in their lives and knows what they need. And these people believe if they do not get what they need, God and their faith will give them the strength to get through the situation. When they do not get what they want, the faithful are often heard saying, "Well, it must all be part of God's plan."

Whether it is part of God's plan or not—we can never know—the faithful draw strength from that belief, the strength they need to get through any difficult situation. It works for them, time and time again. It is at the root of their faith that somehow everything will ultimately be okay. This serves them well during the grieving process.

The Origin of Bargaining and Prayer

Where did all of this bargaining begin? Ages and ages ago, before modern organized religion, we all grew our own food and depended upon rain. If enough rain fell, we had a good year. If not, we had a bad year. Why did enough rain fall one year but not another? People did not know, but they thought some kind of invisible forces must be affecting the weather. They called these forces "spirits" and decided, "If we're nice to them, they'll be nice to us."

People also figured that there were good spirits and bad spirits. That if we're nice to the good spirits, they'll bless us. And that if we ward off the evil spirits, we will be okay. So people came up with different ways to be nice to the good spirits: offerings from the harvest, sacrificing animals (and, unfortunately, people, too), and various other rituals.

And they found ways to ward off evil spirits: by lighting a fire, since they believed spirits lived in darkness and would be scared off by light, and with many other protective actions, objects, and rituals. They also bargained with the evil spirits, which boiled down to: "I'll give up something if you leave me alone."

The remnants of these ways found their way into modern religions, including offering food, sacrificing animals, and using Hanukkah and Christmas lights in place of bonfires. Even circumcision in the Jewish tradition is a form of bargaining: "I'll give you a piece of my son if you leave him alone and do not harm him."

Does all this bargaining work? It is hard to tell. Sometimes it does, and sometimes it doesn't. It works often enough that people still try, they still bargain with God. We believe we have a relationship with God that is similar to having a friend you can rely on. We ask a friend a favor, and we might be granted that favor. Bargaining with God is like asking a friend a favor, even if it is a friend we do not talk to often. The Bible clearly states that when Jonah prayed to God for his release from the belly of the big fish, God commanded the fish to spit Jonah out. Would God have done that even if Jonah hadn't prayed for it? We will never know.

We know from reading stories such as the one about Jonah that God, indeed, does sometimes answer prayers. And that is enough to keep most people from abandoning prayer. On the off chance that God will grant our wishes, we pray and we bargain. We often bargain out of desperation, just as Jonah pleaded with God to get him out of that fish. There's no common sense or logic to it. We will try anything, even if there's little chance it'll work. Why? Because we're in pain.

Bargaining with God implies that we can change God's mind. Theologians have argued about this forever: does prayer change God's mind? Some believe that he is unmoved by our prayers, others believe that he is receptive to them.

In religious services, we pray and we praise God. And it is all just a form of bargaining. Do we pray to God because he asked us to, or is it our idea?

In 70 CE (also called AD), after the destruction of the Second Temple, the rabbis came up with the idea that we should pray to God in place of offering sacrifices, because, with the temple gone, we no longer had a place to sacrifice the animals. Certainly, people had been praying to God since time began, but after 70 CE, prayer became the way to communicate with God, and it remains so to this day in the Judeo-Christian tradition.

Prior to 70 CE, God commanded men to sacrifice animals to him. We see this throughout the writings of the Old Testament. Although God asks for sacrifice (a form of prayer and bargaining), he is not necessarily going to answer by giving us what we want all the time. The Bible is filled with examples of God's giving people what they have prayed for, as well as not giving them what they have prayed for. That sacrifice system, some theologians believe, was simply God's way of saying, "I made you free. This is what you owe me." The same can be said for prayers and praising God.

In this line of thinking, God is asking for us to give back. But you can also give back to the universe in other ways.

You can be a good person without belonging to a synagogue or church, without sacrificing, praying, or praising; simply find meaningful ways to give of yourself to people, to nature and its living resources, to your community, to society, to the world.

There is another way to look at prayer, and it is one you may be less familiar with: prayer is not about bargaining with God, it is about opening yourself up to the universe. The Hebrew word for "to pray" is *lehitpallel*. It means "to judge yourself." So praying is about taking a look at your soul, checking out your soul's condition. Prayers help us do that, because they lead us on the journey inward. Prayer, then, becomes personal, an internalization exercise. This reflects the classical Jewish notion that prayer is not about God—it is about you, and it is about me. It is personal.

I believe that God is no longer all-seeing and all-knowing. He used to be, but he is not anymore. My son, who is an Orthodox Jew, would say to me, "So what difference does that make to God?" He believes that God is still all-knowing and all-seeing. And my son's belief, and his ironic comment, leads directly to this question: does God believe in me?

To help answer all of these questions, we can take a look at a more modern philosophy.

God's Three Laws: A Post-Biblical Philosophy

When God created the universe, it was filled with his glory and his presence, so there was no room for humans to act in the world. Because God wanted to give us a place to be, and to give us free will, he contracted to make space for us. This mystical Judaic notion of contraction is represented by the Hebrew word *tzimtzum*.

In mankind's earlier years, God was far more involved. He made things happen, talked to people, and answered their prayers. He was all-knowing and all-seeing. We see this, throughout the years, documented in the Old Testament. Those were the formative years for his people, so he had to teach them, mold them, and essentially micromanage everyone and everything. Then, eventually, he started pulling back to leave us to our free will.

The idea that God no longer controls everything is a post–Old Testament philosophy that arose because people were looking for an explanation for why God stopped doing the kinds of big miracles we read about in the Old Testament, why he stopped talking to people all the time, and stopped answering very big prayers in very big ways, such as getting the big fish to spit out Jonah. This philosophy says that in the post–Old Testament era, which includes today, God is available to us for guidance, but that he no longer directly controls what happens to us in our daily lives.

If God is not behind everything good and bad, then how and why do things happen? Why does life proceed as it does? Is anyone in charge? To answer that question, we can look to the world that God created and the laws he created to govern that world, to what I call God's Three Laws: natural law, moral law, and historical law.

Natural Law

Natural law covers all the laws of nature. When you throw a pencil up, it always falls down. When a volcano erupts, people are usually going to die. When you get cancer, it could kill you. Natural law is the way the world works, and you can count on it.

In biblical times, everything—good and bad—was considered God's doing. So when Jonah was tossed overboard and swallowed by a big fish, this misfortune was attributed to God's will. And when Jonah prayed to get out of the fish, his release was also attributed to God. However, the post-biblical philosophy of natural law says otherwise.

When someone's father is swallowed by a big fish, or their mother dies of cancer, people ask, "Why did God do that?" Well, God did not do it. He doesn't get involved in such events. It was natural law that did it.

If God is truly in control of everything, it means he made my mother die of lung cancer. And if I believe that, then I am going to be very angry with God because he did that, or did not do anything to stop it. And if I am angry with God, I can't, at the same time, go to God for comfort, in need, and in pain, because I am going to be too angry with him.

God's natural law also covers our free will. People have asked, "How could God have let the Holocaust happen?" Holocaust survivor Elie Weisel's answer is that the question is not how could God let it happen, it is how could *we* let it happen. Hitler had free will just like everyone else, and he chose to be evil. Mother Teresa, on the other hand, chose to be a saint.

People like to believe that God is in charge of everything, because that lets them off the hook. They do not have to be responsible, they do not have to be held accountable, and they do not have to take action.

Moral Law

If you do something wrong, you know it, you feel it, a bell goes off. The first time you do something wrong, the bell is loud and clear. The second time, you do not hear it as well. And the third time, you hardly hear it at all. But you know it is there. It is God. God is your conscience, or your conscience is a part of God. If you add up your conscience, and mine, and everyone else's, you get Conscience (with a capital C): the Collective Conscience of the universe—God.

God gave us moral law to guide us. But we also have the free will to ignore it.

Historical Law

Historical law means there is a purpose and a direction to history, and those eventually lead us back to the Garden of Eden. All of history is the consequence of Eve and Adam listening to the snake instead of God and eating the fruit from the Tree of the Knowledge of Good and Evil. All of our history has been our wandering after our banishment from the Garden of Eden. But history is also supposed to lead us back there. And when we get back there and God says to us, "You may eat from the fruit of all of the trees in the Garden of Eden, except for the Tree of the Knowledge of Good and Evil," this time we will listen to him, because we'll know from experience what happens if we do not.

The Garden of Eden is a metaphor for the perfect world, where we were at one with nature, with God, and with each other. There was peace, no sin, no shame. After God gave us natural law, moral law, and historical law, it was as if he said, "I love ya, call me anytime you want. I am giving you total freedom and free will. Have a nice life. I will be with you, but I do not control history, you, or the world you live in. . . You do."

That means if you are tossed overboard, do not be too surprised if you're swallowed by a big fish. It is one of the risks you take when you go out on the ocean in a boat with a bunch of sailors you don't know. And when someone you love gets cancer, you can try to bargain with God to make that person better, but usually it won't work. But you already know that, don't you? It is not your head that is broken; your head knows that cancer can sometimes kill. But your heart refuses to accept that reality; it always hopes that loved ones can remain with us, that their bodies and spirits will stay healthy and vibrant.

You can go to God, but you can't ask him to change his natural law, and that is the problem with bargaining, why it doesn't work all the time. We can go to God for strength, but not for favors. He can give you strength, but he doesn't do favors, because he doesn't change the laws he gave us. Jonah just got lucky. God could just as easily have said no to Jonah. After all, God said no plenty of other times elsewhere in the Bible.

And, besides, how do we know that the big fish spit out Jonah just on orders from God? Natural law would hold that the big fish's stomach was upset by such a big meal as Jonah and, therefore, did what upset stomachs do. And out came Jonah.

We go to God so we won't feel alone. But if our prayers are answered, so to speak, according to this philosophy, it is God's natural law, not God, that is responsible. If Jonah exits the big fish, if Grandma recovers, if the hurricane bypasses your town, if you narrowly escape an accident, it is natural law operating, not God.

When you are grieving, natural law operates in the same way. When people's prayers are answered, they think God answered them, and that gives them a deeper connection to God. But according to this post-biblical philosophy, they're doing this within the illusion that God directly helped them when it was the outcome of God's natural law that was actually responsible.

Can you still feel a deeper connection to God and thank him, even if you believe it was his natural law that happened to give you a break and not God directly? Sure, why not? After all, God created natural law, and through it Jonah escaped the big fish, enough people recover, hurricanes turn out to sea, and you narrowly escape an accident. And the pain of grief recedes. And then prayer becomes not bargaining but gratitude.

God created everything in the universe. And God created hope.

CHAPTER 2

Death Is Part of Life

THE STORY: To Every Thing There Is a Season, from the Book of Ecclesiastes

⌒

"SHE WAS ONLY a teenager, why did she have to die so young?" "He's been in a coma now for three months, why doesn't God take him already?" Sound familiar? These comments reflect the feeling that we are all supposed to live till a ripe old age, full of life and good health. But it hardly ever works out that way.

The most famous passage in Ecclesiastes is chapter 3:1–8:

> To every thing there is a season, and a time to every
>   purpose under heaven:
> A time to be born, and a time to die;
> A time to plant, and a time to pluck up that which
>   is planted;
> A time to kill, and a time to heal;
> A time to break down, and a time to build up;
> A time to weep, and a time to laugh;
> A time to mourn, and a time to dance;

A time to cast away stones, and a time to gather
stones together;
A time to embrace, and a time to refrain from
embracing;
A time to seek, and a time to lose;
A time to keep, and a time to cast away;
A time to rend, and a time to sew;
A time to keep silence, and a time to speak;
A time to love, and a time to hate;
A time for war, and a time for peace.

We do not know how many moments we get. We also get phases of time, and we do not know how long each of those lasts, either. You do something for a particular length of time. Someone is in your life for a while. You think a certain way for a time. Some experiences and relationships last for a moment, some for one of these phases. Life is made up of these phases of time, and nothing lasts forever.

The passage from Ecclesiastes reminds us that life naturally runs its course. The notion that there's a time for this and a time for that can also be interpreted as: there's a moment for this and a moment for that, and that life is made up of moments.

We mourn the end of these moments just like we mourn a death. They're "little deaths." We mourn the end of a phase, the end of a relationship, the end of one thing or another. We think of losing or leaving these situations and relationships as failing, but this process is not failure, it is simply growth and change in keeping with the seasons of our lives, as this poetic passage shows us.

King Solomon wrote Ecclesiastes in his old age, and he shares the wisdom of his years. He could not have written such words when he was younger, just as we can't grasp the wisdom of experience in our youth. Through these images, he also tells us that you shouldn't hang on to something that doesn't work, and you shouldn't cut off something that does work.

If there's a time for everything, does that mean we shouldn't rush or try to crowd too much into our lives at one time, and should understand that there are stages? Perhaps. I have been a rabbi for more than thirty years, and now I am an author. I was not ready to be an author until now. This is my "season" for that. What season are you in?

Since we mourn the end of our moments, phases, and seasons—some more than others—we must remember that there's a healthy way to mourn them, and we shouldn't let such endings derail us. If the end of the situation or relationship is something we wanted or were prepared for, our mourning will be easier.

We mourn these "little deaths" of situations and relationships by dealing with and going through all of the stages and issues you will find in this book. They do not just apply to mourning someone's physical death.

Death is part of life—not just those physical deaths of living beings, but also those "little deaths" that signal the end of a situation or a relationship.

Ecclesiastes 3:1–8 begins its list with the phrase "A time to be born, and a time to die." King Solomon gets right to the toughest truth first, and he doesn't sugarcoat it. We have a hard time with this concept, because to us death seems to be the opposite of life, not part of it. But death is the last part of life, the end of the life cycle. It can also be simultaneously seen as the first part of our next cycle, wherever we go next.

We're not guaranteed a long life. So we have to get over the idea that death before a certain age is unnatural. You have to literally grieve this idea, because if you are hanging on to it, you can't heal and recover from your losses. If you have the idea that someone died "prematurely" and you can't get past that concept, then you are just adding to your list of losses you have to mourn and let go of. It is hard enough to mourn the person you lost, let alone be saddled with the extra grief you feel regarding what you perceive as the unfairness of the death's timing and circumstances.

If we embrace the idea that death simply happens when it is supposed to happen, then our grief becomes easier. We're calmer and take life as it comes, and we can mourn the loss of the person we cared about without the extra issues that weigh us down.

People say, "You should live to a hundred and twenty." Long life is seen as a reward, and that is what messes us up: if you die before old age, we feel as though you were robbed and cheated.

The further away our society got from living close to nature and its rhythms, the more we grew to think that death was unnatural, that we had to cheat death and try to beat Mother Nature. We turned into a society that fears death, and we became a "life-support society." We can prolong life medically, but at the great cost of quality of life. We see death as a defeat instead of as a natural part of life.

One Last Ride

In the essay "One Last Ride," from his book *Make Me an Instrument of Your Peace* (San Francisco: HarperSanFrancisco, 1999), author Kent Nerburn writes about one woman's graceful last ride, and the man who gave it to her:

> There was a time in my life twenty years ago when I was driving a cab for a living. It was a cowboy's life, a gambler's life, a life for someone who wanted no boss, constant movement, and the thrill of a dice roll every time a new passenger got into the cab.
>
> What I didn't count on when I took the job was that it was also a ministry. Because I drove the night shift, my cab became a rolling confessional. Passengers would climb in, sit behind me in total anonymity, and tell me of their lives. I encountered people whose lives amazed me, ennobled me, made me laugh and made me weep. And none of those lives touched me more than that of a woman I picked up late on a warm August night.
>
> I was responding to a call from a small brick fourplex in a quiet part of town. I assumed I was being sent

to pick up some partiers, or someone who had just had a fight with a lover, or a someone going off to an early shift at some factory for the industrial part of town.

When I arrived at the address, the building was dark except for a single light in a ground-floor window. Under these circumstances, many drivers would just honk once or twice, wait a short minute, then drive away. Too many bad possibilities awaited a driver who went up to a darkened building at 2:30 in the morning.

But I had seen too many people trapped in a life of poverty who depended on taxis as their only means of transportation. Unless a situation had a real whiff of danger, I always went to the door to find the passenger. It might, I reasoned, be someone who needs my assistance. Would I not want a driver to do the same if my mother or father had called for a cab? So I walked to the door and knocked.

"Just a minute," answered a frail and elderly voice. I could hear something being dragged across the floor. After a long pause, the door opened. A small woman somewhere in her 80s stood before me. She was wearing a print dress and a pillbox hat with a veil pinned on it, like you might see in a costume shop or a Goodwill store or in a 1940s movie. By her side was a small nylon suitcase. The sound had been her dragging it across the floor.

The apartment looked as if no one had lived in it for years. All the furniture was covered with sheets. There were no clocks on the walls, no knickknacks or utensils on the counters. In the corner was a cardboard box filled with photos and glassware.

"Would you carry my bag out to the car?" she said. I took the suitcase to the cab, then returned to assist the woman. She took my arm, and we walked slowly toward the curb. She kept thanking me for my kindness.

"It's nothing," I told her. "I just try to treat my passengers the way I would want my mother treated."

"Oh, you're such a good boy," she said. When we got in the cab, she gave me an address, then asked, "Could you drive through downtown?"

"It's not the shortest way," I answered quickly.

"Oh, I don't mind," she said. "I'm in no hurry. I'm on my way to a hospice." I looked in the rearview mirror. Her eyes were glistening. "I don't have any family left," she continued. "The doctor says I don't have very long."

I quietly reached over and shut off the meter. "What route would you like me to go?" I asked. For the next two hours, we drove through the city. She showed me the building where she had once worked as an elevator operator. We drove through the neighborhood where she and her husband had lived when they had first been married. She had me pull up in front of a furniture warehouse that had once been a ballroom where she had gone dancing as a girl.

Sometimes she would have me drive slow in front of a particular building or corner and would sit staring into the darkness, saying nothing.

As the first hint of sun was cresting the horizon, she suddenly said, "I'm tired. Let's go now." We drove in silence to the address she had given me. It was a low building, like a small convalescent home, with a driveway that passed under a portico.

Two orderlies came out to the cab as soon as we pulled up. They were solicitous and intent, watching her every move. They must have been expecting her. I opened the trunk and took the small suitcase to the door. The woman was already seated in a wheelchair. "How much do I owe you?" she asked, reaching into her purse.

"Nothing," I said.

"You have to make a living," she answered.

"There are other passengers," I responded.

Almost without thinking, I bent and gave her a hug. She held on to me tightly. "You gave an old woman a little moment of joy," she said. "Thank you."

There was nothing more to say. I squeezed her hand once, then walked out into the dim morning light. Behind me, I could hear the door shut. It was the sound of the closing of a life. I did not pick up any more passengers that shift. I drove aimlessly, lost in thought. For the remainder of that day, I could hardly talk. What if that woman had gotten an angry driver, or one who was impatient to end his shift?

What if I had refused to take the run, or had honked once, then driven away? How many other moments like that had I missed or failed to grasp? What if I had been in a foul mood and had refused to engage the woman in conversation?

We are so conditioned to think that our lives revolve around great moments. But great moments often catch us unawares. When that woman hugged me and said that I had brought her a moment of joy, it was possible to believe that I had been placed on earth for the sole purpose of providing her with that last ride.

I do not think that I have ever done anything in my life that was any more important.

Let that sink in. Read it again if you'd like. The woman in this essay, and the man who took her on her last ride, approached the natural end of her life with dignity, open hearts, and peace.

The Blame Game

You've probably heard the phrase "Only the good die young." We console ourselves by theorizing that God wants the good people with him, and takes them sooner than he takes everyone else. We know enough wonderful people who died young (and enough nasty ones who live to a ripe old age) that even the most rational among us suspect that this theory might be true.

If we give up the assumption that we're going to have a long life, we might think we will be closer to God, because if we think we could die at any moment, we will constantly bargain and pray for more time. But that would be an artificial relationship with God, not genuine closeness. That is merely using God out of fear.

Some people think if a child dies, God has either made a mistake or is punishing someone. We've often heard grieving parents say, "What have I done that God is taking my child? God is punishing me." We shouldn't think this way. Unfortunately, old Bible stories reinforce this kind of thinking, because in those tales God was constantly taking people away as punishment. How do we reconcile our believing in a "good God" with the possibility that God may be punishing those we love when he brings death to them? How do we know when someone is dying as a punishment from God and when they're not? In the Bible, God gave the death penalty for what we'd consider some pretty tame offenses. In those days, if you ticked off God, you were dead. But on the other hand, in biblical times, as well as today, God apparently let a lot of people live after they had committed some pretty despicable crimes.

One answer can be found in God's Three Laws, the post-biblical philosophy I commented upon in chapter 1. According to this philosophy, God doesn't kill people now, natural law does. In Biblical times God was more directly involved in everyone's life, and he did kill people, but not today. He created his Three Laws, and one of them, natural law, is what actually kills people.

Even those who believe in this philosophy can still end up exactly where those who *do not* believe in it end up: looking for someone to blame. People think they feel better when they have someone to blame, but assigning blame never really helps and it makes no sense. It is not real, it's just an illusion that temporarily acts as a Band-Aid. We believe if we can hold someone accountable—even if that "someone" is God—then we will feel that justice has been served. Even if the wrong person or the wrong idea is blamed, we still feel better.

Blaming God, or anyone else, when they've got nothing to do with what's happened is not real, but what also makes people feel better when they play this blame game is that it gives them someone or something to rage at. It lets them be heard.

Unnatural versus Natural Death

Even when death is unnatural, it is natural. Since none of us gets out of here alive, every death is essentially natural, because it is normal to die. It's just the circumstances that we sometimes consider unnatural, and that is because of our unrealistic expectations concerning what's natural and what's not. Ironically, what's considered unnatural is really pretty darn natural. Let's take a look.

You may think it is unnatural to die in a certain way— after being shot or when you jump out of a plane and your parachute doesn't open. Well, guess what—it is not at all unnatural to die after being shot. And don't you think it is pretty natural to die when you hit the pavement after falling hundreds, if not thousands, of feet from the sky? It would actually be unnatural to survive a hail of bullets or the long plunge to earth that ends with you going *splat* on the pavement.

We need to change our perceptions, because they're wrong. They're backward. And they cause us pain. We must strip away all of this unnatural versus natural silliness so that we're simply mourning the loss of our loved ones, not also dealing with the pain of our unrealistic expectations and ideas about what's natural and what is not. Get rid of this angst that twists your mind in knots and gets in the way of grief recovery.

The only entity who lives forever is God. God is immortal, people are not. Even if you believe in reincarnation, you still die after each life. Your soul goes on, but you are still someone who dies and will be grieved in each lifetime. Your soul is contained in a human body, and that body doesn't live forever. Everyone's container is going to die. Whether you call it unnatural or natural, death comes when the body can no longer sustain life. And that is a perfectly normal thing for the body to do.

What's Your Mission? It May Not Be What You Think

There's a theory that everyone has a mission, and that when your mission is accomplished, you are finished—you die. I'd like to believe the mission theory. The interesting irony of this theory is that people usually don't know what their mission is. They think they do, but they're usually wrong. That is because your mission is usually something a whole lot smaller in obvious, outward scope and a whole lot more inwardly focused and profound.

Your mission can be said to contain one key lesson that you are supposed to learn while you're alive. When you die, you may not even be aware that you've accomplished your mission. But other people may have figured it out if they were paying attention.

Pamela was paying attention. Back in the nineties her friend, whom we will call Allie, had been missing her husband, who was working out of town for a number of months. At first Allie had a hard time being on her own, and then one day she said to Pamela, "I don't feel lonely." A month or so later, Allie, barely into her thirties, died in a car accident.

Ten years later, Pamela's divorced mother, Mary, who had always been uncomfortable if she was not part of a couple, had been having stomach pains. When Pamela telephoned her mother and asked how she was doing, Mary replied uncharacteristically, "I don't feel lonely." A few days later she was in the hospital with septic shock and a bleak prognosis. After surgery, which the doctors were surprised she survived, she clung to life on a respirator for two weeks, and then she died. Mary was sixty-two.

After her mother died, Pamela thought back to Mary's shocking words, "I don't feel lonely," and remembered that Allie had said the same thing just before her fatal car accident.

All of their lives, Allie and Mary had found it emotionally difficult to spend time on their own, not in the company of men. In fact, Pamela knew that her mother had made many life choices based more on avoiding being on her own than anything else. "I think that Allie's and my mother's missions, their lessons, were the same. As soon as each of them finally felt genuinely okay being by themselves, they died," Pamela says. "They'd each accomplished their life mission, though I'm sure that neither one of them would've ever thought that was what they were here to learn, to accomplish."

Think back to the people you know who have died. Perhaps you will find clues to each of their soul's life missions or lessons in the days, weeks, or months before their deaths.

The trigger for learning your lesson—accomplishing your mission—is always your response to a loss in your life. Loss is always somewhere in the equation, even if what you are losing is some preconception or pain you've carried around all your life, or some incorrect idea of who you really are or what you really need. You lose that and grow. You "see the light," so to speak. You have an epiphany, an "A-ha" moment, a lightbulb moment. You finally "get" something, you understand it. Finally, light is shed on something. Lesson learned, mission accomplished, now you can go. You've grown to a new phase of life—your death.

When people have near-death experiences, they often see a bright, loving light waiting for them. As much as they would like to go to the light, they're not allowed. They're told, or they sense, that they're being sent back to life because they haven't yet completed their mission. It could be said, then, that once you've seen the light here, you are welcomed into the light over there.

My Best Friend

One of the most dramatic examples of this mission and lesson phenomenon can be seen in the life of Rabbi Kenny Berger. Kenny and I grew up together, we were like brothers, and he was the closest friend I've ever had. We met in a Jewish youth group when I was in high school in Philadelphia, then went to summer camp together and became counselors together. We both became rabbis and continued our close friendship as adults.

In January 1986 the Challenger space shuttle blew apart shortly after liftoff, killing all of the astronauts on board. After an exhaustive investigation of the accident, it was determined that after the explosion the astronauts were alive for five more minutes. Kenny wondered what they had been thinking about during those last minutes when they all knew they were going to die. He wrote a sermon about this and delivered it from the pulpit to his congregation on Yom Kippur in the fall of 1988. Rabbi Berger said in his sermon that people who know their death is imminent probably have three thoughts in common during their final moments, and each of the three begins with the phrase "if only."

> If only I had known when I said my last good-bye to the people I love that it was my last good-bye.
> If only I realized what I had while I had it.

If only I had another chance, then I would do
it better.

In the months that followed, from the fall of 1988 to the
summer of 1989, Kenny's sermon circulated through the
country and was quoted both in print and in the congregations of close to one thousand rabbis. Kenny's synagogue
offered him a lifetime contract. At only forty-one, he would
have the ultimate job security, an offer that many rabbis would
love to have. But Kenny wouldn't have been happy at one synagogue for the rest of his life. Would he accept their offer?

On July 19, 1989, Kenny, his wife, and his two young
children boarded a plane in Tampa, Florida, to fly across
the country for a visit with his wife's family on the West
Coast. Back home, that as yet unsigned lifetime contract
with the synagogue waited for him on his desk. About
halfway through the flight, the plane had mechanical problems and the pilot told everyone to prepare for a crash
landing. As the plane spiraled downward, Kenny had time
to think about his life. He had time to think about those
three "if onlys" that he'd spoken of in his now-famous
sermon. The plane crashed in Sioux City, Iowa, killing
Kenny and his wife. Their two children survived.

What do we make of the irony that Rabbi Kenny Berger
died in a manner identical to what he'd written in his
sermon, and that he died just before he was supposed to
sign a lifetime contract? Kenny's lesson—his mission—
was to learn those three lessons he wrote about, have time
to do them so that he wouldn't approach his death with

any "if onlys," and have time to teach this lesson far and wide before he died. That is why there was a gap of time between his sermon and his death.

Would Kenny have signed that lifetime contract? Did he die precisely when he did—before signing the contract— because he would have signed it and ultimately would have regretted that decision? Ironically, he did end up spending the rest of his life at that synagogue. It is just that the rest of his life did not last very long.

Kenny didn't know that the lessons he had taught in his sermon were his life's mission, his life's major lesson, and that soon after he'd accomplished that mission and achieved his "A-ha!" lightbulb moment, he would die. The same goes for me, and you, and everyone else. If you think you know what your mission is, and think that if you do not complete it you can postpone your death, just remember that it might not be your true mission and lesson. Do not bother trying to cheat God or Mother Nature. Most likely something else is your mission, and you will accomplish it not knowing that is what it was, and that you will soon leave this life.

Your life may be short or long. Either way, when you die, by definition you will have accomplished your mission. When children die after long illnesses, we often hear their parents say that those children taught them love and compassion. Apparently, that was their mission. Once it was accomplished, they left. If you look at the entertainment business, the people who live the longest are comedians. Maybe their mission is to bring as much insight, joy, and laughter to people for as many years as possible, for as many years as their bodies can hold up.

If you are skeptical about this life mission/life lesson theory, if you think it's just coincidence or just so much superstitious mumbo-jumbo, remember the life of Rabbi Kenny Berger.

Making Every Pitch Count

In his e-mail newsletter, *Your Life Support System* (available at www.lifesupportsystem.com), author Steve Goodier shared a story that reminds us to live our lives to the fullest while simultaneously letting go of our worries about dying one day:

> One night, a Dodgers farm club coached by Tommy Lasorda was leading Tucson by one run in the eighth inning, but Tucson had the bases loaded with two outs. According to Don Martin in *TeamThink* (Penguin Books, 1993), Lasorda decided to pep up his pitcher, a left-hander named Bobby O'Brien. Lasorda slowly walked out to the mound and said, "Bobby, if the heavens opened up right now and you could hear the voice of the Big Dodger in the Sky and he said to you, 'Bobby, you're going to die and come up to heaven, and this is the last batter you're ever going to face,' how would you like to meet the Lord, getting this man out or letting him get a hit from you?"

"I'd want to face him getting this guy out," O'Brien replied.

"That is right," said Lasorda, "you would. Now, how do you know that after you throw the next pitch you're not going to die? This might really be the last hitter you're ever going to face and if it is, you'll want to face the Lord getting him out."

Lasorda figured it was just about the best pep talk ever and he strutted confidently back to the dugout. O'Brien wound up and threw the pitch. The batter lined a base hit to right field, knocking in two runs.

Lasorda was beside himself. "Bobby, what happened?" he asked.

"It's like this, Skip," said O'Brien. "You had me so worried about dying I couldn't concentrate on the batter!"

Many people are worried about dying. Their worry can keep them from fully enjoying life in the present. But for other people, the knowledge that they will die someday actually motivates them to live more fully!

Dr. Elisabeth Kübler-Ross, who has extensively studied death and dying, put it like this: "It's only when we truly know and understand that we have a limited time on earth—and that we have no way of knowing when our time is up, will we then begin to live each day to the fullest, as if it was the only one we had."

It's true, we have no way of knowing when our

time is up. But we have today. Will you live it as if it were the only day you had?

When You Accept That Death Is Part of Life, What Will Your Life Look Like?

Some people are keenly aware that death is part of life, because they consciously face the possibility of death every day. It is just another aspect of their jobs as firefighters, police officers, miners, soldiers, and other professions that require more bravery than usual. They have a certain mind-set that we can learn from, and so do their loved ones. On any given day, death is not a guarantee for them, it is just a possibility, but they have accepted that. For many of the rest of us, it is guaranteed that one day we will die, but we haven't accepted that very well.

We think the odds are high that something could happen to those who have dangerous jobs, but we do not think the odds are high that something could happen to *us*. Of course, that is not true. Any one of us could drop dead at any time or die in an accident, but we do not see it that way. In a sense, maybe that is a good thing, because if we thought of ourselves as possibly dying every time we walked out of the house, we'd never walk out of the house.

So we have to find some healthy medium. What would that be? Functional paranoia? Is that the mind-set of firefighters and their families? I don't think so. I think the healthy medium is awareness and acceptance without fear. And if we have that, what will our lives look like? Perhaps we will make better choices. Perhaps we will seek and value the wisdom that can come from growth and maturity.

Wisdom means knowing that the choices you made before (although some may have seemed right at the time) are not the choices you would make today. You only learn that through loss and grief. Some people become wise earlier than others. When they've had enough of the outcomes of choices that led to loss, they become wiser about their choices. Hopefully, these segments of our lives—these moments, phases, and seasons—give us wisdom. We learn from each and apply what we've learned to the next moment, phase, and season.

If you lost someone, or more than one person, when you were young, how did that change you and how you live? When you hit middle age, more of your friends and family die. If you've been through that, did those losses prompt you to change how you live?

Even one small change is meaningful. With each death, we change. All those deaths add up to a lot of changes over the years. So death actually leads us to life! A different life, a wiser life, a better life. A life filled with more life than we had before.

"To every thing there is a season, and a time to every purpose under heaven: A time to be born, and a time to die." I think about those words every time I walk out of a cemetery after a funeral (and a rabbi conducts a lot of funerals), and I am reminded that since any one of us could die at any time, we have to live fully every single moment. We do not know when our time will come.

CHAPTER 3

Tragedy

The Story: Lessons from the Book of Lamentations

❧

SOMETIMES GRIEF affects an entire community, a country, a nation. When it does, the grief is perhaps even deeper than when it comes to just an individual. If everyone is mourning, who will be there to help us? In the Old Testament book of Lamentations, the people of Israel are lamenting a great tragedy: the 586 BCE destruction of the First Temple, in Jerusalem, and the aftermath, when the Jews were exiled from Israel—taken as prisoners of war—to Babylonia.

Lamentations is attributed to the prophet Jeremiah, who is said to have written part of it before leaving Israel and part of it while in exile in Babylonia. What came before, during, and after the temple's destruction was a bloody nightmare, and Lamentations is filled with despair. Nobody believed their lives could ever get better. In Lamentations 5:15 Jeremiah looked at the devastation and wailed: "Gone is the joy of our hearts; our dancing is turned into mourning." This is the reaction that people have to every kind of tragedy.

We can draw strength from knowing that others have recovered from tragedy and loss. The first step is expressing your grief—lamenting—and Lamentations shows us exactly how to do that. We can imagine anyone in the middle of a war, or any other similar tragedy, saying what Jeremiah wrote in Lamentations:

"Bitterly she [Jerusalem] weeps in the night, her cheek wet with tears. There is none to comfort her of all her friends" (1:2). How appropriate this quote is to the experience of those in Europe who went through the Holocaust.

"Zion's roads are in mourning, empty of festival pilgrims; all her gates are deserted" (1:4). This quote could just as easily be expressing the feelings people had about New York in the immediate aftermath of 9/11.

"For these things do I weep, my eyes flow with tears: far from me is any comforter who might revive my spirit; my children are forlorn, for the foe has pre-vailed" (1:16). We can imagine any parent in a concen-tration camp or modern-day refugee camp crying and mourning with these words.

"My eyes are spent with tears, my heart is in tumult, my being melts away over the ruin of my poor people, as babes and sucklings languish in the squares of the city" (2:11). Pick a country, pick a modern or historical war or tragedy, and these sentiments apply. Those who mourned twenty-five hundred years ago were no different than we are today.

The last verse of Lamentations, 5:21, says it all: "Take us back, O Lord, to yourself, and let us come back; renew our days as of old!" This means, *Please make everything like it used to be*. And if that is not a reaction to tragedy, I don't know what is.

The Challenges of Mourning a Tragedy

Tragedy is always a wake-up call; it always reminds us that we weren't prepared enough or that we could not prevent it, and that is why so much guilt accompanies any tragedy. However, instead of wallowing in guilt, we should see guilt only as an effective signal to prepare for the future and to do something that may prevent this kind of tragedy from happening again.

After a child drowns, for example, the people who were responsible for the child feel guilty, angry, and have a difficult time with forgiveness. But they're dealing with very specific circumstances that can help others prevent such a tragedy in the future: perhaps the child was left unattended, or a gate was left open, or there was no gate. When they look at the particulars of the situation, they can clearly see how to prevent another such tragedy, and this often helps those who are mourning. It gives them a tangible focus for their pain, but it also gives them a tangible focus for their forgiveness, healing, and grief recovery.

We hear about so many people who use the pain of their tragedy to inform others and to work at preventing these tragedies from happening to others. Larger-scale tragedies—wars, bombings, attacks, genocides—though, are more complex, and it is a challenge to identify their components as the focuses of pain, forgiveness, and healing. Preventing these tragedies is also far more challenging.

In tragedy you have plenty of company in your grief, many people also grieving as you are who understand exactly what you are going through. This is an important source of comfort. But it is also a trap, because you can get even more stuck in your grief when everyone around you, often an entire geographical area, is also grieving and there's little normalcy in your environment to help you begin to heal. You and the other grievers can keep going 'round and 'round in your grief like water swirling down a drain.

Learning from a 9/11 Survivor

The survivors of tragedies often have added difficulties during every part of the grief recovery process. We can learn from the experience of a man we'll call Bob who survived the collapse of the World Trade Center towers on 9/11.

Bob had spent decades working for New York City, and loved his work. By the time of 9/11 he had an upper-level management job with the city, and its safety was never far from his mind as his responsibilities included plenty of interaction with the Office of Emergency Management as well as the police and fire departments. "I was treated as one of them," he recalls. "It was a nice relationship."

Prior to 9/11 the worst problems any of the city's employees—at any level—ever had to deal with were emergencies such as small fires and minor flooding. They had plans in place for many kinds of emergencies, "But 9/11 went way past what we were trained to do," he says.

On the morning of September 11, 2001, Bob had just left his Midtown Manhattan office and was on his way to an appointment when he got a radio call at 8:49 AM saying that "a small plane hit the tower," he recalls:

> Nobody got excited at first. I kept in contact with all of my people downtown, then got a call on my cell phone from the Office of Emergency Management, and I headed downtown, because they were setting up the evacuation of the tower. I was on the West Side Highway and saw the second plane hit. I was scared. I wasn't sure what else was going to blow up! I didn't know the impact the planes made until I got downtown. I went inside the first one that got hit, Tower 2, on the ground floor, where the city's command center was set up. Nobody had an idea that these buildings were going to come down. I never had the fear that the buildings would come down.

Bob's biggest concern was that he would walk out and be hit by debris falling from the burning tower, or that other buildings might be hit. Working now at the command center in Tower 2, he, like everyone else, wondered what might happen next. "Earlier, when the second plane hit, I knew it had to be terrorists. I thought we were at war with somebody," he recalls. "I was a smoker at the time and was running out of cigarettes, so I wanted to go out to my car and get another pack." One of his colleagues, a close friend, said he'd go with Bob to the car, where there were also some fresh batteries for the radio. So the two men left the command center at Tower 2 and headed for the car.

"I was parked a block away from the building," he recalls. "I was just opening the door to my car when I heard the most incredible sound I'd ever heard. I didn't know what it was until I looked up. The top of Tower 1 was coming down—Tower 1 came down first—and I looked for a few seconds, then I dove under the car." His colleague dove under the car as well, "and we held hands like two babies, praying. It only took a few seconds for the building to come down. It got darker, colder, grayer. If that is what hell is like, that is about as close as I want to get."

Under the car, the two men were shielded from large pieces of debris, but were completely covered by a grayish-white coating of ash and fine particles of debris. "We both thought we were going to die," Bob says, still filled with the emotion of that day. "He was praying to Jesus and Mary, and the only Jewish prayer I could remember was the

Shema. Somebody was watching over us. To this day, I'm not sure why I'm here."

But he did survive, and so did his colleague. "When everything became still, we came out from under the car, backwards. We'd come in head first, so we slid out with our feet in the street," he recalls. "There was the most incredible smell that I'd never smelled before—they say it was the poisons in the air. I couldn't see anything. It was like a gray, heavy fog had set in. We started walking away from it. We were in shock. Everything solid had turned into a powder, a dust, but you could see a full sheet of paper flying around, with company letterhead, and not a singe on it."

After walking a couple of blocks, they saw firemen at an intact fire truck on the street. They stopped and washed themselves off. Bob walked up to Fourteenth Street, to the closest city bus garage, and made some phone calls. "The cell phones weren't working and the land lines were hit and miss," he remembers:

> I had a bite to eat, and got another set of clothes from the Red Cross there. Now it was all about survival. I thought we were at war, so it wasn't just about a job, it was very personal. I wanted to save my family and myself. My mom was in her eighties, and I knew she'd be in another world about this. When I called her at about 1:30, she said, "How do I know you're okay?" I knew how relieved she was. Then I called my wife. She was in her office in Jersey; she'd been sitting at her

desk watching the TV they brought in. The first thing I said was "I love you." She wanted to know how I was, and I told her that I was okay, that I was just dirty. I didn't tell her what happened until many months later.

Bob made his way back to his Midtown office, which became one of the city's command centers. "We had police, fire, and EMS communications there," he recalls. "The next six to eight hours were chaotic. It was like a zombie world. You've gotta realize how close the mayor came to being wiped out. Nobody thought these buildings were going to come down. I've always realized how short life can be, and this just reinforced it. Don't wait 'til tomorrow to do something you can do today, because tomorrow may not come."

The love that poured out from New Yorkers and to New Yorkers astounded him. "The city opened up," he says. "People were out in the street morning, noon, and night, with water, sandwiches, anything anybody wanted. The city had a heart. I think the city went seven or eight days without even a purse snatching."

For the next three months Bob worked seven days a week, going home to New Jersey once or twice a week. "There were a lot of heroes," he says. "People get these rushes of adrenaline, and they're ready to do whatever they need to do."

The images of what happened to the towers haunt him, but they also fill him with compassion and pride. "It was so hot up there, the helicopters couldn't land on the roof of these towers to rescue anyone," he explains:

If you know you're not going to live, to be in that much torture and know that you have to escape the inferno you're facing—I think the people who jumped had so much courage. They knew they weren't going to survive. Jumping had to be better than staying, which is very scary to think about. What they had to be feeling—I can't even imagine the pain they were going through. I saw one of the people who jumped, saw one come down, as I was walking into the tower. And then to see firemen racing into the building, going up when everyone else was coming out . . . Even after the buildings came down, we had hope that we'd find people alive.

He mourned the loss of so many people. The funerals came one after another, and another. One in particular stood out. "They did a funeral for a Port Authority cop's dog," he remembers. "And they gave the dog the funeral of an inspector, because the dog was the cop's partner."

For about three months after 9/11, Bob went to see the city psychiatrist. "It was mandatory for anybody who was that close to it," he says. But those sessions did not help much. "The thing that really saved me was going up to our house in the woods at Thanksgiving that year. I spent about five days there by myself, just me and the animals. I think that saved me."

Bob took early retirement about eight months after 9/11 and hasn't been back to New York City since. He and his family moved from New Jersey to their vacation home in another state. "When I retired, I came up to the house myself first, and I don't think I came off the mountain for three months. I went to the supermarket and that was it," he remembers:

> That was the best therapy for me. I was able to get rid of all the medications; I stopped having the nightmares. I used to wake up screaming in the middle of the night that things were falling down. Now I'm working on my temper. I've always reacted, but since 9/11 I overreact. And I have a hard time, still, with how people could hate other people so much. We're all here on borrowed time; it's a gift. I wake up, see the sun, and I'm thankful that I have another day.

They were close friends before 9/11, but ever since that day, Bob and the colleague with whom he hid under the car share a survival bond that continues. "We talk to each other every September 11th," Bob says. "It's our private time together."

Talking about It Always Helps

And in fact that is precisely how we survive tragedies—we talk to one another and share our stories. I remember where I was on November 22, 1963, when John F. Kennedy was assassinated, as does everyone in my high school. I was home sick that day, watching television, when all of a sudden the live reports came on the air. At our last class reunion, we talked about those awful days, and each of us remembered exactly where we were at the time. The same goes for the 2001 attack on the World Trade Center. The words "9/11" have become a symbol of tragedy in America, and we remember where we were and what we were doing when the planes struck. Talking about grief, whether personal or communal, always helps. It is why we Jews tell stories during shiva, the seven-day mourning period after the funeral. We talk, we listen, we cry, and we laugh about the one who has died, and it is that talking that somehow makes it a little better for us all.

Commemorating Loss and Tragedy

Every year on 9/11 Bob and his former colleague commemorate the tragedy of that day in 2001, as well as their harrowing experience. This is their private commemoration, and they do it because it is human nature to mark the meaningful events of our lives. Tragedies, in particular, trigger our strong need for commemoration, immediately after the events as well as in the future, usually on anniversary dates and the birth dates of those associated with the tragedies. People put flowers, candles, photos, messages, and religious icons at the spots where loved ones have died in car accidents and at public spaces or the homes of those who have died in any number of other ways. Remember the sea of flowers in Great Britain when Princess Diana died? And those in front of John F. Kennedy Jr.'s New York City home after he, his wife, and sister-in-law died in the crash of his private plane?

People want to mark a tragedy in a long-lasting way, too, by building memorial structures and creating holidays and private and community rituals, as well as music, books, movies, cards, you name it. The AIDS Memorial Quilt that was started in 1987 was one such creation. We commemorate as a way to make sure people do not forget, and to make sure they always remember the people and the lessons behind the tragedies.

The three elements necessary for any commemoration are *time, community,* and *ritual.* A *time* that is relevant to the tragedy is chosen, usually the anniversary or a relevant person's birthday. The tragedy is then commemorated over time, usually annually. Although you can also mark such occasions alone, commemorations require *community:* other people remembering the same tragedy on the same day as you are. The commemoration always includes *rituals,* those special things we do each time to mark the occasion.

Sometimes it is difficult to decide how to commemorate a tragedy. Look at all the controversy surrounding choosing the proper structure to build on the World Trade Center site. This is part of the natural response to tragedy. It is hard to figure out the right way to commemorate a tragedy. Sixty years after the Holocaust, we still do not have an agreed-upon liturgy to mark the event. The only ritual that has been agreed upon, so far, is the lighting of six candles on Yom Ha Shoah, the annual Holocaust Remembrance Day, to commemorate the death of the six million Jews.

Commemorating is an important part of the healing and grief recovery process, because it is how we focus on healing, and it's how we end each tragedy.

"Renew Our Days as of Old"

The book of Lamentations ends with the plaintive wail: "Take us back, O Lord, to You, and let us come back; renew our days as of old!" (5:21). We will see what happens at Ground Zero. No one knows what the future holds, but we do know that the future will look nothing like the past. It can't—the past is gone forever, never to return. Commemorating the past is an important piece of our grief recovery; we need to remember, talk about, and commemorate the tragedies of our lives, so that we will then be able to focus on building a new future.

Part Two

AND GOD CREATED HOPE

CHAPTER 4

Shock and Anger

The Story: The Death of Aaron's Sons, from the Book of Leviticus

$\frown$

SHOCK IS THE first response to a sudden, unexpected death, but even an expected death leaves loved ones and others feeling numb. It is a perfectly natural reaction. This chapter addresses the results of this shock: how long it lasts, how we function while we're in emotional shock, how we get through it, and its aftermath.

On the very day that Moses's brother, Aaron, was made a high priest, God killed Aaron's two sons, Nadab and Abihu, because they took it upon themselves to make an offering of burning incense, even though God hadn't commanded an offering from them. When his two sons were so suddenly killed, Aaron's first reaction was silence, shock, and numbness.

Aaron was also silent when God killed his sons, because he understood why they had died: it was a natural consequence of their actions, regardless of whether that consequence—death—was too severe a punishment or not. In his head he was quiet, but in his heart he was in shock. It is one thing to consider that God could kill for this kind of seemingly small offense, but it is quite another for it to happen to your own sons. Perhaps Aaron was also silent because he did not want to challenge God and be the next to die.

His sons' deaths also might have been one of Aaron's lessons about what his role as high priest meant: how important it is to follow God's rules, and how Aaron would need to relay this to people. Another lesson? That the high priest's children aren't excused from God's rules. Aaron got that lesson loud and clear. And it contributed to his shock.

But Aaron was also human, and his sons had just been killed, even though it was by God. Nevertheless, Leviticus 10:3 says, "And Aaron held his peace." In Hebrew the word *vayidom* is used, which means silent as well as numb and dumbfounded. When we're in shock, like Aaron, we're also shocked by the death's circumstances and implications. After his sons died, what did Aaron do? Even though he was in shock, he kept functioning. He was the high priest, after all, and he had responsibilities. He never said a word about his sons' deaths. But staying silent was wrong. And we can learn from Aaron about what not to do.

Do not stop talking about loved ones who have died. Although it was good that Aaron continued fully with his life and his work, it was not good that he never mentioned his dead sons again. No one can heal when they keep their grief to themselves. Talking about those who have died is integral to the grief recovery process. To stay silent is like pretending the deceased never even lived, never had an impact on your life. Such silence is a form of denial, and only serves to clog up the emotional drain. Talking about those who have died is a healthy venting, a healthy flow through the emotional drain.

When you're in shock, it helps to be with people. It's like a reality check. They're in shock, too. You can be compassionate with each other, and by talking to each other the death begins to sink in and the shock begins to slowly wear off.

While he was in shock, we can safely assume that Aaron was also upset about the end of the hopes, dreams, and expectations he had for his sons, about the end of their futures.

Aaron's shock had to be spiced with a good deal of anger. Anger at God, anger at his sons—even, perhaps, anger at himself. He would have been angry with God for killing them, angry with his sons because they would have still been alive if they hadn't made that offering, and angry with himself because he wondered if he could have done something to prevent their deaths. When we're in shock, we react the same way—with anger, frustration, and plenty of "if onlys." In grief, shock and anger always go hand in hand.

Aaron never let his anger out. We can learn from that, too. Learn what *not* to do. Do not keep your anger in. Let it out in a safe, appropriate, private setting among those who understand you and will comfort you.

Perhaps the most shocking part of Aaron's story is that despite everything that happened, Aaron continued to be a high priest and didn't walk away from God. Does this speak to Aaron's capacity for forgiveness? Or does it mean that Aaron feared God so much that he just silently went along with him? Perhaps Aaron understood God's actions and considered his sons a sacrifice. Leviticus never sheds any light on these questions, because Aaron's sons, their death, and his reaction are never mentioned again after that one sentence: "And Aaron held his peace."

What Else Shocks Us?

When someone dies, what ideas and circumstances can shock us? The list is always long and tailored to the particular person who died, as well as the griever who's in shock, but here are some of the most common elements of that list:

- The idea that the person died "before his time."
- That he died in a particularly gruesome way.
- That she died "out of the blue" without warning.
- That he died right in front of you whether it was expected or not.
- Believing that he died "unfairly," such as through an accident; murder; from the side effects of medication that was supposed to help him; after a surgery that was expected to go well; after first seeming to get better; just before or after a joyous occasion, such as engagement, marriage, a child's birth, graduation, professional achievement, an honor or

award, meeting a personal goal, an anniversary, birthday, or holiday; being in the wrong place at the wrong time and becoming the victim of a natural or other kind of disaster; and the like.

- Being alone for the first time or after spending many years with the loved one who died.
- Feeling overwhelmed by having to take care of all of your life's practical and logistical obligations when you've been used to sharing those tasks or having someone else do all of them.
- Being angry that someone else is not shocked or angry about the death and its circumstances and effect on you.

The Second Shock

Shock is like a one-two punch. The first shock is when the person you care about dies. The second shock is when you realize that she is not coming back—she is really gone.

Sometimes the second shock comes soon after the first, but often it can come weeks, months, or even years after the first. Especially if this is a mourning without death, if you are grieving a loss such as divorce or the end of a relationship. At some point after the initial breakup, when you realize that she is not coming back, that is your second shock.

The second shock can be even bigger than the first, because often the real, deep mourning can only begin after the acceptance of loss that the second shock represents. It's finally sinking in . . . it's over. Whether by death or breakup, it is really over. She's gone. She is not coming back.

You grieved after the first shock, and maybe you even thought you were pretty far along in your healing process, when, *WHAM!,* the second shock hits you and you find yourself grieving even harder than when you first got the bad news.

This is part of what makes the grief recovery process so complex: you have to grieve over and over again. This isn't something that a lot of people talk about, because most people mistakenly think that once you grieve over someone, you're finished. But that is not true. At any point during the healing or recovery process you can feel like you are starting all over again, mourning from scratch.

Hello, New Orleans

I have loving cousins who live in New Orleans. They, like many other people, had to evacuate their home and city during Hurricane Katrina in late August 2005. Fortunately for them, we have family in Atlanta, so that is where they went. Together with Rochelle and Bobby, there is their son, Justin, a high-school junior, and my elderly aunt Lil, who is in her nineties. Rochelle, Bobby, and Justin moved to a residence hotel, and Aunt Lil moved to a senior citizen residence. After a year, they decided to return to New Orleans. Aunt Lil remained behind in Atlanta.

Wow, I thought, *is this a good decision or not?* First, to move back to New Orleans meant moving back to a city that is still not fully functioning as it needs to in order to support those who live there. Would there be enough government services? Police? Fire? Schoolteachers? It turns out that the main reason they decided to move back is so that Justin could resume classes with his friends. After all, they had been in school together for eleven years, and he wanted to be back with them in comfortable, safe, and familiar surroundings.

The neighborhood where they now live is on higher ground, so the damage there from the hurricane was minimal. But they have moved back home to a city that still has lots of problems. There is no downtown. The city is in shambles; it hardly looks or even sounds like the New Orleans they once knew and loved. Power is still off in many neighborhoods, and hospitals are not yet fully staffed. The question can honestly be asked: *What kind of future will they now have?* Why move back at all? Maybe staying in Atlanta would have been a better way to go.

On the other hand, I suspect that most of those who left New Orleans will by now be experiencing their "second shock." First, their city was destroyed and no one came to help them, so they had to leave. That was the first shock. By now they are feeling like strangers in communities that are not their own, surrounded by caring and loving people who have reached out to help, but who by now are probably feeling something like, "Okay, it's been nice to have you for a while, we're glad we could help you out when you needed us, but now please leave us alone so we can get back to our former normal lives."

This is a natural and normal feeling on the part of those who took New Orleanians into their homes, schools, factories, and communities. Here comes the second shock, where again there is a feeling of being an alien in a strange land. So I can well understand Rochelle saying that they wanted to return home to New Orleans. Their home is their haven, and they missed it terribly. By the way, Aunt Lil is doing great in the Jewish Home in Atlanta—who would have thought? She has neighbors, staff to take care of her, food she likes, and nearby relatives to come and visit, so she is very happy. I'm sure all of this made Rochelle's decision much easier.

What is the right answer? Should they return to New Orleans or stay in Atlanta? I have no idea. I feel sad for my cousins and their friends who return; they are living in the middle of a dilemma with no solid solution. On the other hand, I guess that is what hope is—in the midst of ambiguity, the courage to move forward and to make a conscious decision that no matter what, there is a bright future to look forward to. And that is how Rochelle sounds on the phone whenever we talk. Good luck, my cousins, and good luck to all those who are coming home.

The Benefits of Shock

Immediately after receiving the bad news, shock can actually be good for you, because it protects you from the initial intensity and reality of losing someone. Shock fortifies you and allows you to deal with the loss gradually as the shock wears off. The shock temporarily paralyzes you, in a way, and that can protect you while you let the reality sink in and begin the early stages of healing at your own pace.

The numbness you feel is like the Novocain the dentist gives you so you don't feel him drilling into your tooth. By the time the numbness wears off, the healing has begun and you are beyond the sharpest, initial pain. The shock and numbness has protected you from feeling as acutely as you would've felt if you had not been numbed by shock. As the numbness wears off, you've been gradually acclimating to the pain.

Getting through the Initial Shock and Anger

There's not much you can say to people that will comfort them immediately after someone dies. They're too much in shock for anything to help. In fact, the Talmud says you shouldn't say anything to people when "their dead are lying before them." Instead, just hug them and comfort them. Nothing you say, other than "I'm sorry," or "What do you need?" is going to help, and the wrong words can be damaging.

How do you get through shock? Gradually. First, you think about the next moments, then the next hour, then the next twenty-four hours. You get through day by day. You focus on what you need to do each day. Incorporating some of your regular routine helps, because routine is good for you when you're in shock—it centers you and makes you feel somewhat normal in the midst of what feels abnormal about your days: your shock and grief.

Don't try to deny your feelings, and do not try to deny that you are in shock or that you're angry. Denial never helps; it just makes everything worse.

Do not be surprised if you're angry. It is only natural, since anger can result from feeling abandoned, frustrated, and sad. When you acknowledge your anger, guilt may surface. It is not uncommon to feel guilty about being angry. But there's no need to feel guilty, since you've done nothing wrong. There's nothing wrong with feeling angry that you've lost someone. It is a perfectly healthy emotion to feel at this point in the healing process.

Your anger may also be directed at the one who died (or whom you lost in a relationship), doctors, God, or anyone else for any reason. Anger can actually be a positive force in the early stages of your grief, because it's a sign that you value yourself. When you're angry in this situation, it is a way of saying, "I did not deserve this; I am entitled to a good life, to this not happening to me."

Anger helps us believe that the world is ruled by order. We're angry because we feel that life has deviated from how it should have been: we weren't supposed to lose a loved one.

Although anger can be healthy, excessive and prolonged anger can turn into revenge, make you lash out at others, and lead to depression and even thoughts of suicide. Anger projected outward leads to violence. Anger projected inward leads to self-destructive behavior.

When You are Angry with God

Recently I received a phone call from a man whose father had just died. His mother had died not long before that, after battling cancer for several years. Before she died, she had stopped coming to the synagogue, because she was angry with God. She felt that God had deserted her and had stopped taking care of her, so she was going to stop visiting him at the synagogue.

Her son and I had a long talk about all of this. When I suggested to him that his mother's anger at God had been a perfectly normal reaction, he was surprised. He thought that most people maintain their faith in God, no matter what.

I believe that is not the case. I believe that most of us have a fairly fluid faith—when life is good, we believe, and when life is not so good, we do not. We become angry with God when we're afraid we will lose, or have lost, loved ones. We become angry with God when we fear for our own lives.

When we were infants (if all went well), everyone took care of us—our parents, older siblings, other family members, and our doctors. We didn't have to make any decisions, and our lives were in the capable hands of others. When we grew up, however, we realized that we had to take on the responsibility for our lives and make our own decisions. No longer could we depend upon others to keep us safe. That was now our job. But when illness or impending death enters our lives, we want to return to what life was like in childhood. We want to again rely on others to take care of us, make us well, return us to life.

When our doctors and caregivers, in whom we place so much hope, do help us, we feel safe again. But when they can't fix our illnesses, we become angry. We know that these people are only mortal human beings who are doing the best they can, and we know that the human body has its own agenda, which no one can change. Still, we are angry.

Sometimes our anger is directed at God, whom we'd like to believe can "do anything," even cure incurable diseases. Our heads know the truth, but our hearts do not, and they break when pain overwhelms us.

Our anger is normal, but it isn't pure anger. It is filled with fear. When we have to change the way we've lived for so many years, when we become homebound or need bedpans and walkers, when we have to depend on dialysis and adult diapers, when we spend too much time in the hospital and we begin to realize that our lives are coming to an end, we're scared. That fear comes out as anger. The anger we feel is the fear that we no longer have a life to enjoy, and that death is coming closer with each passing day.

I think most of us let God into our lives only when we're afraid. God is the force in the universe that gives us the hope that allows us to move forward when we feel like giving up.

No matter how many days, weeks, or months we have left to live, we have the ability to make decisions about how we live and what we want to happen before we die.

The ability to look beyond pain is one of the precious gifts God gives to us. Even when we're filled with fear—or, perhaps, especially when we're filled with fear—God walks with us, just as he did when we were infants in our parents' arms. God will be with us always. All we have to do is believe.

Shock Frees or Freezes You

When you've lost someone, the shock either frees or freezes you. Initially, shock freezes every griever. Some are afraid they'll stay frozen. Most, though not all, will "thaw out" and become free.

During shock's initial frozen stage, you begin to discover what you're made of. You call upon your inner strength, resilience, and coping skills in order to move from frozen to free. Some people are stronger, more resilient, and better able to cope than others.

When someone is physically freezing, we put a blanket on him. The emotional equivalent of a blanket is community, compassion, and time. The community aspect can be tricky, since community is interaction with people, whether it is a few people or many. Because each of us has a different healing style, after a loss some grievers need to be alone for a while before they're ready for a whole lot of community. They need time alone to begin adjusting and sorting things out. These people heal better when they have some time away from others.

Taking time alone to heal is healthy as long as it doesn't turn into hiding. One day you might be in the mood for a few people, and the next day you might feel better with more people around you. Then the day after that you might want to be alone. This is only natural. If you are the kind of person who heals better with more time alone, you may look frozen on the outside, but you are actually free on the inside.

Other grievers avoid dealing with loss by jumping right back into their full routine, going back to work right away, and surrounding themselves with lots of people all the time. These grievers aren't healing; they're using unhealthy avoidance tactics. This is just a busy-looking version of being frozen: the griever looks free on the outside but is actually frozen on the inside.

The younger or less resilient you are, the more likely you will believe you should be surrounded by a lot of people when you're in shock and in the early stages of grief. The older or more resilient you are, the more you might want fewer people around and more time to yourself, because you are more emotionally self-reliant, and you've discovered from past experience that when you're with a lot of people, you have to deal with their well-meaning, but often annoying and draining, ways of trying to console you— ways that aren't consoling at all, and usually filled with advice that you know doesn't apply to you. You end up spending all of your time and precious little emotional energy defending and explaining yourself to other people.

Some people who try to console you end up just slowing down your healing. They don't mean to do that, but they just don't have the knack for consolation. They think they should say something, and it's often the wrong thing. When you've lost a loved one, the last thing you want to hear is, "Well, it's probably for the best." And even the most faithful among us aren't necessarily consoled by the words, "She's with God now, so everything's gonna be okay." With all due respect to God, mourners would really rather have their loved ones alive and with them.

When you are grieving, you just want consolation and comfort, not necessarily advice and opinions. But most people don't know how to console and comfort. They mistakenly believe that advice and opinion are synonymous with consolation and comfort, but they aren't.

Mourners need to be heard. When you are mourning, talking and telling your stories helps you go from frozen to free. You are not necessarily looking for those who are listening to say anything useful or wise, but people find it hard to just sit there and say nothing, so they respond, and those responses can often be useless or upsetting. Seek out only those people who can truly comfort you with their actions or words—or silence.

What does it look like when shock and grief freezes you? One day, about twenty years ago, Barbara stood on one side of the street and told her nine-year-old son, who stood across the road, that it was okay to cross the street and come to her. Just as he entered the street, a speeding car came out of nowhere and hit him. A week later, he died in the hospital.

Despite the loving efforts of her husband and her other children, Barbara never recovered from the shock. She just withered away. When her son died, her life stopped. His death "killed" her, too, even though she was still breathing and walking around. Compounding the shock of seeing a car slam into her son was the guilt she felt. After all, she had told him it was safe to cross the street. And what makes it even more difficult when you lose a child is that from that point on your child's death becomes not only your internal identity, but your external identity as well. People say, "Oh, there's Barbara Whose-Son-Died." You get a new last name. Barbara had led a charmed life; she had been happy and had a happy family, but the shock of losing her son froze her.

What does it look like when shock and grief free you? Not long ago I spoke with a teenage girl who, five years ago, had found her mother's body after the woman had committed suicide. The mother had been a single parent who'd been depressed for many years, and the girl had played "mother" to her.

This strong, resilient teenager used the shock and grief of her mother's death as a springboard to a better life. She's now in college, living on her own, and working to support herself. She has a brother, but she's no longer in touch with him because he's a drug addict who won't accept any help, so she's on her own. She's happy, healthy, and independent because she's finally out from under the responsibility and weight of a dysfunctional family. The shock of her mother's suicide five years ago ended up freeing her: it opened the door to her healthy new life.

The woman who'd had a happy life was frozen by the shock of losing her son. The teenage girl who'd had a difficult childhood was freed by the shock of losing her mother. Perhaps the woman with the picture-perfect life had never gone through any experience that triggered the development of any meaningful coping skills. Perhaps the teenager's difficult childhood had made her more resilient. Perhaps the more you've been tested by pain, the better you get at surviving it, and the better the odds that shock and grief will not leave you frozen.

Thinking back to the biblical story of Aaron, I wondered whether he had been frozen or freed. Did Aaron's shock ever wear off? Did he heal? I figured he had probably stayed frozen.

I asked some of my fellow rabbis what they thought, and Rabbi Peretz Rodman, a writer and educator in Jerusalem, had a most profound answer. "I'll tell you what I think: I don't know," he wrote me. "And isn't there a useful message in that, too? Often, we cannot know whether, or to what extent, the people we are dealing with—certainly in casual or business contexts, maybe even at home—have healed after grief. That means that we have to be very careful in what we say, conscious of how it might reawaken their pain."

Of course he is right. You and I might assume that someone we're talking to or working with is in good shape after a loss, when in fact they're still in shock. The person may look fine on the outside, but who knows what's happening on the inside? We really have no idea. And it is that not knowing that ought to stimulate our compassion. Never assume anything; instead, ask the person who is grieving and hear what they have to say. Who knows? Perhaps your kindness will help that person become a bit less angry with the world, and their healing will come a bit sooner. Perhaps they were waiting for someone just like you to come along and invite them to talk about their shock and anger. You did, and they did. Now you have given them a dose of hope, and for that you both will feel grateful.

CHAPTER 5

Ritual

The Story: The Burial of King Asa, from the Book of II Chronicles

ONE OF THE ways we mourn is to rely on ritual. Ritual means routine, something that happens time and time again, you can count on it. Routines can become an antidote to the out-of-routine death that we have just experienced. An example of an ancient ritual can be found in the Old Testament story of King Asa, who reigned over Judah, one of the two kingdoms of Israel, for forty-one years, from 867 to 908 BCE, when he died. A description of his burial ritual can be found in II Chronicles 16:14: "And they buried him in his own sepulchres, which he had hewn out for himself in the city of David, and laid him in the bed, which was filled with sweet odours and diverse kinds [of spices] prepared by the perfumers' art; and they made a very great burning for him." He was buried in an above-ground mausoleum in Jerusalem, laid out on a bed filled with perfumes and sweet spices. Then he was honored with a large bonfire close by.

King Asa's people engaged in this ritual to honor their king. No doubt it comforted them to participate in a traditional farewell ritual, to give him a "sweet" burial, followed by a spiritual and celebratory show of light.

Ritual plays a central and helpful role in our lives and a very important role in mourning, the grief process, and healing.

Ritual Matters

Ritual first alerts the community that something of importance has happened. Then it invites the community to join in the ritual, and by doing so, it creates and strengthens the sense of community among people. Ritual means you do not have to navigate the universe from scratch or reinvent the wheel each time something happens. You know automatically that "this is what we do" when someone is born, someone is sick, someone comes of age, someone gets married, someone dies, plus scores of other kinds of occasions.

Rituals mark rites of passage, large and small, but they're also incorporated into daily life. In our society, even such seemingly mundane events as registering to vote, obtaining a driver's license, and going to the dentist are infused with ritual. But so is putting on your pants. We call our daily rituals our routines. And the way we put on our pants is one of our routines—we do it the same way every day without even thinking about it. Left leg in first, or right leg in first, you do it the same way each time. If you do not believe that you are hooked on your routines, tomorrow morning try putting the opposite leg in your pants first, but make sure you're near your bed so that when you fall over you won't hurt yourself!

When I go into a parking garage I always park on the top level, no matter what the weather. That way I don't have to think about where I parked when I come back looking for my car. Ritual is like that—it simplifies our life. Ritual makes us feel safe, it gives order to the events in our lives, and it gives importance to particular events.

We don't like it when our rituals, our routines, are broken. People who regularly go to church or synagogue tend to sit in the same seats week after week. We seek comfort in the familiar, so we feel comfortable with our rituals and routines. No surprises, no concerns about what we're going to do, what's going to happen, just reassuring automatic pilot. Rituals reduce anxiety and the chances that the unexpected will happen. What we like about ritual is that we know exactly what to expect. So those who walk into church or synagogue and find other people in their seats stop in their tracks, a bit disoriented. Suddenly they realize they have to think and make a choice: *Where should I sit?* They're not used to doing that when they walk through the door. They're a bit annoyed. It is a small thing, but it shows us the power of ritual and routine.

Community ritual encourages you to do something you may not take the time or trouble to do at home. Think of all the people who wouldn't do yoga, work out, or exercise at home, but will go to a yoga class or to the gym.

They go to a place specifically designated for this ritual, and everyone else there is doing the same thing. It is familiar, and they know what's expected from them. If it's a class, someone else is leading, and they have very few decisions to make. They do not have to think, they just have to follow. And it feels empowering to be with other people who are all engaged in the same rituals, all doing the same thing at the same time.

"Ritual is fundamental for human beings because it forms structures of social coordination. Rituals are very important for coordination of time and social relations between people. Without ritual in its most basic sense, there would be no social life," explained Dr. Bradd Shore, the director of the Emory University Center on Myth and Ritual in American Life, in an interview that appeared in the autumn 2000 issue of the Sloan Work and Family Research Network of Boston College's *Network News*.

> Second, ritual is a form of social memory, it is how we remember who we are. It may be that when people are thinking back to their family life or to their time as children, it is the existence of ritual events that provide memory points, and a lot of things that aren't ritualized are forgotten. People go back to: "When we got together for Thanksgiving, or Christmas, or graduation ceremonies . . ." Ritual is fundamental because it provides structures of memory. A third part of ritual is meaning-making and updating meaning in people's lives. Living rituals always combine traditional content, which

is repeated year after year, and a forum by which people update meanings in their lives in new, distinctive ways.

The Empty Chairs

They were filled once with the loved ones who have been a part of our holiday meals for as long as we can remember. Some were our grandparents, some our parents, some spouses and siblings, and some our beloved children. Last year they were sitting right there in "their" chairs, next to us, laughing and celebrating. How should we respond to the empty chairs, to the emptiness that fills our hearts with such sadness? Holidays are supposed to be such a time of joy, but how can we be joyful without our loved ones who are now gone? Their chairs are empty, and our hearts are filled with heaviness. What do we do?

We have lost something profound, and we must realize and verbalize this loss. We have lost our loved ones, those who have taught us, raised us, and been our role models and teachers. They are gone, we are left to go on without them, and it hurts. They were connected to our lives for so long, and now suddenly they're not here. A part of them still lives inside us.

And we have lost even more. We have lost the order and the familiarity of sitting down together, in the very same seats that we sat in last year at this time. We felt safe and comfortable, everyone was in their correct chair, all was right with the world. But now the order is all wrong. The seating is different, because different people are sitting in those chairs. When our loved ones die—or divorce out of the family—we are adrift, without rudders to guide us. Not only do we miss them, but we also miss the certainty of the familiar. Who will sit in Papa's chair this year? How could anyone fill his chair, or his place in the family? When a matriarch or patriarch dies, the family roles are now also adrift. Who will be the next family leader? Who will chart the family's emotional direction, who will be the histo-rian, who will be the family spokesman? Who will we call when a family crisis occurs? Death affects us in countless ways, many of them coming to the surface at our holiday celebration times.

What shall we do? How can we begin to create a "new normal" for our family? A first step is verbalizing our feel-ings of loss. At the beginning of the holiday meal, why not take a minute or two to remember those who are not with us this year? Go around the table and tell stories, laugh together at the good times of the past, cry together at the profound loss. Make the pain public, and share the past so that you can then begin to create the future. Those you have lost may not be with you in person, but they will always be with you in spirit. Make their spirits a part of your family's holiday meals, and your loved ones will live on in your lives for as long as your memory of them lives on. Then you will have found and discovered one of life's great secrets—you are still alive! You can still be vibrant, passionate, and committed to yourself and your family. Life will be different without those you have lost, but you will help create a new life that will bring you and your family a new order, a new familiarity, a new sense of power and creativity. And that is certainly worth a holiday celebration.

Are You a Ritual Kind of Person?

When it comes to ritual, there are two kinds of people: those who like ritual and those who do not. I think we're probably hardwired to either like ritual and feel we need it, or not like it and feel we don't. So it's difficult to get a ritual person to let go of ritual, and to get a non-ritual person to embrace it. And we shouldn't try. Let people be who they are; let them meet their needs according to what works for them.

The people who like ritual feel that it helps them connect spiritually or emotionally to something or someone. They need the symbolism or routine of ritual to serve as a bridge and make them feel connected.

The people who do not like ritual believe it is a barrier, that it stands in the way of the natural, just-born-that-way, spiritual or emotional connection they feel with everything. They prefer to experience their direct connection without anything symbolic in the way. Ritual annoys them. These people are creative, and they feel that ritual removes spontaneity, flexibility, and creativity from the picture. They want to express themselves with flexibility and creativity, and ritual stifles that. To these people, ritual feels stagnant, passionless, a meaningless going-through-the-motions. Even if you told them they could create their own rituals, they still wouldn't embrace the idea. Any rituals they would create would have to be open to continuous change. These people do not want to do the same symbolic routine over and over. That does not comfort them.

Those who like ritual often feel they can't connect without it. It is a necessary path or bridge for them. It also gives them something to do, and it comforts them in the midst of the often uncontrollable, unpredictable, and mysterious. These people aren't particularly comfortable with change or the unknown, so ritual makes them feel safe.

Some people who like ritual do not have any spiritual connection at all. All they have is ritual. These people do not understand others who don't like or skip the rituals, and mistake them for being "un-spiritual," or "un-believers," when, in fact, those who don't need or particularly like ritual are sometimes the most naturally spiritual among us.

Ritual and Mourning

Traditional mourning rituals tend to be classified by religion and culture, since those two institutions are an important part of our major rites of passage: birth, coming of age, marriage, and death. Every religion has a ritual for each rite of passage, and even people who do not consider themselves particularly religious will usually participate in their religion's ritual during those rites of passage.

Traditionally, Christian mourning rituals take place before the funeral: people come to the funeral home to view the deceased at a visitation or wake. A wake also includes a celebration of the deceased's life at a church, someone's home, or a public place.

Jewish mourning rituals take place after the funeral: Jews "sit shiva" after the funeral and interment. Shiva begins the night of the funeral (that is considered the first day of shiva) and ends the morning of the seventh day. Jews do not sit shiva on the Sabbath. Shiva is the weeklong mourning period that brings mourners, friends, and family together at the home of a close family member of the loved one who died. Its purpose is community, so the mourners are not alone. People are welcomed into the home to visit during the day or in the evening. Prayers are said during short services at the home at specific times each day. One of those prayers, Kaddish, is said on a number of occasions, including during the funeral, during the shiva services, every Sabbath during the mourning period (eleven months if you are mourning a parent, thirty days if you are mourning anyone else), and on the anniversaries of the loved one's death.

One Jewish ritual that happens before the funeral is not considered part of the official mourning period that begins with shiva. It is called *tahara,* the ritual preparation of the body before the funeral and burial, which is per-formed by members of the community, but never the deceased's family. All Orthodox Jews, as well as some Conservative and Reform Jews, go through the ritual of *tahara* before they're buried. Even some of those Conser-vative and Reform Jews who do not observe the ritual will request one particular aspect of it: that someone stay with the deceased from the time of death until burial so the deceased won't have to be alone. You will learn more about *tahara* later in this chapter.

Ritual gives us something special to do on special occasions. If that occasion is a death, ritual is a way to honor, remember, and show respect to the one who died. Ritual can often be a way we feel we're giving our loved ones a send-off to the great beyond. It is our time to think about them, and we hope they know—wherever they are—that we're thinking of them. It's common to feel their presence at the funeral and during other rituals, even if it's just because we feel ourselves connected to them by thinking of them, talking to them in our heads, and praying for them.

Ritual is also the main way we publicly show grief. We participate in official rituals, public and private, but when we mourn we also create our own rituals based on what has meaning to us and to those we've lost. Because these rituals are very personal they can be especially healing and can play an important role in closure. People often mark closure with a ritual, even if they do not think of it as a ritual; for example, the wife who finally clears out her late husband's closet a year after he died. She can do this, finally, because she has closure. Taking his clothes out of the closet is a ritual that symbolizes that closure.

Rituals always signify something, because they're usually symbolic. Which ritual we undertake and when we do it are based on what we're trying to express, so ritual is also a form of communication. Clearing out her husband's closet is a widow's symbolic way of saying, "I'm better now."

When King Asa's people lit the bonfire in the city after they put him in his final resting place, it was to signal God that Asa was coming to be with him. People also lit bonfires in those days to scare away evil spirits. Fire, as a signal and a protection, has always been used in a variety of rituals and celebrations. Today we might set off fireworks.

I spoke with a mourner who went to a memorial service for a friend who had died suddenly and unexpectedly. After his memorial, a few of his friends went outside and set off fireworks. He had loved fireworks, so this was their personal ritual to honor him. But it was also a way to let off some steam and make some noise. It is an acceptable way of screaming when you're grieving, by letting the fireworks make the noise you would like to make.

Many other symbols abound at memorial services, including helium balloons that are released outside to signify the soul's flight to heaven.

Expressing our grief can be challenging in most modern cultures, because we've been conditioned to hold in our feelings, especially in public. It was not always that way. According to Savine Gross Weizman and Phyllis Kamm, authors of *About Mourning: Support and Guidance for the Bereaved* (New York: Human Services Press, 1985), "We have given up the rituals which sanctioned the full expression of grief and denied mourners the opportunity for catharsis of their grief."

Thankfully, for those who need them, some rituals live on.

Hevra Kadisha: Learning from a Ritual Experience

The first time I ever touched a dead body was shortly after I arrived at my first pulpit, in the fall of 1976. One night the chairman of the congregation's Hevra Kadisha—which means "holy society"—called me.

"Rabbi, someone has just died. Can you meet me in the morning at the funeral home for *tahara?*" he said.

He was asking me to help prepare the body for burial, which is what the members of Hevra Kadisha do.

"Sorry, I do not do that," I replied.

"There's no one else," he said.

So I went. And that was the beginning of my fascination with the Hevra Kadisha and the ways we Jews approach death.

I'd learned about the Hevra Kadisha in rabbinical school, but I never thought it was for me. Who needs to touch dead bodies? They're intimidating, even a bit scary. Little did I know then that the Hevra Kadisha would turn out to be my passion for the next thirty years, and counting. There's nothing gruesome about it, and I believe there is no more compassionate way to serve those who have died and those who mourn them. And no more holy way to serve God.

Although preparing bodies for burial in a traditional Jewish manner goes back thousands of years, the Hevra Kadisha is a relatively modern institution. The first ones were organized in fourteenth-century Spain and Germany. The first community Hevra Kadisha began in Prague in 1564, and, unlike the earlier groups, which served only their own members, this new group's services were available to all members of the Jewish community.

This ritual begins the community's process of letting go. And if you're a member of a Hevra Kadisha and prepare the body of a member of your community, it prepares you to begin the letting-go process when one of your own loved ones dies.

Today, many communities have their own Hevra Kadisha groups. Although most large North American cities have a community Hevra Kadisha sponsored and organized by a local funeral home that caters to the needs of the entire Jewish community, sometimes the Hevra Kadisha is sponsored by a single synagogue and its services are available only to members of that synagogue. All Orthodox Jews who die go through *tahara* before burial. More and more Conservative and Reform congregations are now creating their own Hevra Kadisha groups.

Usually, we members of the Hevra Kadisha gather at the funeral home the evening before a funeral. If the deceased is a Hevra Kadisha member's relative, that member will not come.

We prepare ourselves for our holy task with words of prayer, and then together we enter the *tahara* (which means "purification") room. Men prepare men, and women prepare women.

Before we uncover the deceased person, we ask his or her forgiveness for any indignity that might accidentally occur. We then wash the entire body twice, first for physical cleanliness, then for spiritual purity. This is the final journey, so we must make sure he or she is well prepared.

After drying the body, we dress it in a simple white linen shroud. Every Jew prepared by the Hevra Kadisha is buried the same way now, but that has not always been so. In ancient times the rich were treated much better than the poor, and in response the rabbis established rituals that resonated loudly with the belief that every human being deserves equal treatment from birth through burial.

The notion of democracy in death is illustrated best by the following quotation from the Talmud, Moed Katan 27 a–b:

> Formerly, they used to bring food to the house of mourning: the rich in baskets of gold and silver; the poor in baskets of willow twigs. The poor felt ashamed. Therefore, a law was established that all should use baskets of willow twigs. Formerly, they used to bring out the deceased for burial: the rich on a tall state bed, ornamented and covered with rich coverlets; the poor on a plain bier. The poor felt ashamed. Therefore, a law was established that all should be brought out on a plain bier . . . Formerly, the expense of the burial was harder to bear by the family than the death itself, so that sometimes they fled to escape the expense. This was so until Rabban Gamliel insisted that he be buried in a plain linen shroud instead of costly garments. And since then we follow the principle of burial in a simple manner.

After the body is dressed, the members of the *hevra* lovingly carry the body to the coffin and place it inside. A man is buried in his own tallis (prayer shawl), with one of the tzitzit (fringes) cut off and placed beneath the pillow. A small bag of earth from Israel is placed beneath the pillows of both men and women as a symbol of the connection every Jew has to the land of Israel. The coffin is closed, not to be reopened. Once again members ask for forgiveness from the deceased, and *tahara* is completed.

We do not leave the dead unattended, however. Someone stays with the body from the time of death until burial. It is an additional mitzvah (blessing) for a member of the *hevra* to sit with the deceased the night before the funeral. One person doesn't stay all night. This is usually done in three-hour shifts, and there is always spiritual material to read. The next day is the funeral, and the Hevra Kadisha's job is finished.

There are two overriding principles that govern Jewish traditions and rituals of mourning: respect for the dead and respect for the living. Both before and after death, these principles offer both an overview and a theological lens through which details can be understood.

Jewish tradition is firm in its respect for the dead. The human body is God's gift to us and must be treated with dignity at all times, even after the soul has departed. After death, the body is handled respectfully, because it is the repository of the soul. Nothing may be done to the body, and no procedure may be performed that disfigures it in any way, except under the most controlled of circumstances.

Autopsies are, for the most part, prohibited, unless civil law dictates. But if a rare disease caused the death, Jewish law requires an autopsy to help save the life of the next person who might be afflicted by that disease.

For the same reason, a Jew is prohibited from donating his or her entire body to medical science, because it is unavoidable that the body will be mutilated in a medical school setting. Donating individual organs, however, is encouraged. Saving a human life is the highest priority in Jewish tradition, so donating organs is admired as a great act of mercy and compassion for God's creatures.

I have been a member of the Hevra Kadisha in many places, and I've had the honor of creating Hevra Kadisha groups in three synagogues. I've learned much about life and death, about how we reach upward in holiness each time we participate in a *tahara,* and about how ordinary people can perform extraordinary acts of caring and kindness. The Hevra Kadisha has been my teacher in many ways.

As a ritual, it provides an echo of God's presence and gives us the opportunity to imitate the works of God. As God buries the dead, so we bury the dead. As God consoles the emotionally and spiritually troubled, so must we. As God acts with justice and compassion, so do we. As God cares for us, so we care for others, even after their lives in this world have come to an end. Indeed, by doing so, we remind ourselves that when our own times comes, God, perhaps in the form of a future Hevra Kadisha, will continue to care for us.

When I finish preparing a body and leave a funeral home, I am filled with gratitude: once more I stand in the presence of death, and once more I'm privileged to walk away, still alive, still able to serve God and his creations.

Performing *tahara* is an echo of pure compassion. This aspect of Hevra Kadisha is perhaps the most appealing to its members. In the outside world we expect some reward for almost everything we do. The notion of reciprocity is a common part of our society. How refreshing it is to be with volunteers who are passionate about being able to give freely of themselves to someone else, simply because that is the tradition. The mitzvah, the blessing, itself is its own reward. Because no one outside the Hevra Kadisha knows our identities, we serve with no possibility or expectation of public accolades.

Although many Hevra Kadisha volunteers say that they first joined because they were asked to do so, they remain because they feel they're carrying on a compassionate traditional ritual. Many members feel that the respect for the human body that is evident in *tahara* is the most moving aspect of the process. Some compare *tahara* to caring for an infant. That idea has allowed some to overcome their fears of handling the deceased. Some members feel that this is one last favor they can do for the deceased, and that helps provide closure.

It is perfectly normal to feel a bit queasy and uncomfortable about handling a dead body. Many people believe strongly that they can't do it. I know that feeling. I felt the same way thirty years ago. But this unease is often quickly overcome when we remind ourselves why we are there. When you let the mitzvah speak to your heart, your fear soon disappears.

There is a hunger for spirituality that can't always be met in our daily activities. The Hevra Kadisha touches the very edge of life. It offers us not only a glimpse of death, but also an echo of eternity.

The Power of Ritual

Ritual brings people together, and it can help you grieve, heal, and recover, but it can also be used inappropriately. People squabble over ritual all the time. Within each religion, people make judgments based upon what those rituals are, who's participating in them, and to what extent. And who's not participating. Some Conservative and Reform Jews view Orthodox Jews as "too Jewish" because of the Orthodox Jew's rituals. And, of course, some Orthodox Jews think Conservative and Reform Jews "aren't Jewish enough," because they do not perform most of the Orthodox rituals. Some Christians view others as "too Christian" or "not Christian enough" based on similar judgments about beliefs and ritual. People of one religion, or one culture, or one country, or one race get their ideas about people of other religions, cultures, countries, or races by looking at their rituals.

Ritual, then, is very powerful. And like all powerful ideals it can be used to heal or to harm. Anything that can heal you (including medical treatments) can also potentially hurt you. When you are in pain and grieving, rituals can hurt you when, out of desperation, you look to extreme religious groups and cults that promise you that everything will be okay as long as you participate in their rituals. You are especially vulnerable when you're grieving, and such groups can seduce you with their rituals: they "love bomb" you and give you the illusion of comfort and safety in return for giving over your power to them.

You can take ritual too far when you're mourning. (Nobody takes ritual too far when they're getting married. They're not vulnerable, they're not in pain.) In chapter 9 you will read about how one man's grief led him to a breakdown when his extreme emotional and psychological vulnerability left him open to take ritual too far.

Celebratory rituals are different than consoling rituals, but all rituals, if you use them as a crutch, can be emotionally harmful if they keep you from healing. Rituals are a corridor to healing and can be extremely helpful. In any loss situation, and in particular a death, when we feel our total lack of control over life and death, rituals may give us back a sense that we are still in partial control. That control is limited, but important to us nonetheless. When the Israelites built a bonfire in memory of their departed king, they were making a statement—we loved him, we will miss him, and his light will never be extinguished. And that is a feeling worth honoring.

CHAPTER 6

Fear

The Story: The Golden Calf, from the Book of Exodus

⌒

WHEN SOMEONE DIES, we are left alone, physically and often emotionally as well. What do we do now? How do we adjust to being without that loved companion?

God commanded Moses to meet him at the top of Mt. Sinai. Moses went, leaving the Israelites to wait for him at the base of the mountain. They had been slaves in Egypt and had been free for only a few months, so they had little experience with freedom. With their leader, Moses, away on the mountain, they felt uncomfortable and afraid. When a few weeks passed and he still hadn't come back, the Israelites feared he might never return. Where was he?

The Israelites panicked. They felt abandoned. They felt they had to do something. So they went to Moses's brother, Aaron, and asked him to make them a god. With Moses gone—maybe for good, they feared—they wanted the security of knowing someone (or something) was going to take care of them. Aaron asked the Israelites to give him their gold earrings, and they did. He melted down the gold and made them a Golden Calf to worship. They were thrilled. They felt safer. They offered up sacrifices to their new god, they danced, and celebrated.

Meanwhile, back up on the mountain, God had already given Moses the Ten Commandments, one of which forbids worshipping any other gods, including idols like the Golden Calf that the Israelites were now worshipping at the bottom of the mountain. God was not happy. "Go down there," he said to Moses. "Your people are acting badly. They're worshipping a Golden Calf they call God!"

So after forty days and forty nights on Mt. Sinai, Moses finally came back down to the Israelites. Carrying the two tablets on which God had inscribed the Ten Commandments, Moses stood before his people and watched as they celebrated and danced around the Golden Calf.

Moses was furious. He hurled the tablets at the foot of the mountain and they shattered. Then he destroyed the Golden Calf.

God was even angrier and killed many of the Israelites. God then commanded Moses to go back up to the top of Mt. Sinai to receive another set of tablets. Moses went.

After another forty days and forty nights on the top of Mt. Sinai, Moses returned to the Israelites and presented them with the Ten Commandments. When they heard the commandment that forbids worshipping idols or other gods because there is only one God, the Israelites understood why their worship of the Golden Calf had so angered Moses and God.

Understanding Fear

Fear is normal. Fear is not the problem. The problem is the unfortunate choices we often make when we're afraid—such as making an idol and praying to it, whether that idol is a Golden Calf or any modern-day crutch we create or use.

What do we fear when we anticipate the loss or death of a loved one? What do we fear when we're grieving that loss or death? The list of fears seems endless:

- Fear of the unknown.
- Fear of pain.
- Fear of being alone.
- Fear of never feeling good or happy again.
- Fear of the loss of love.
- Fear of the loss of emotional security.
- Fear of the loss of financial security.
- Fear of your routine "normal" life being shattered, and not knowing what kind of life will replace it.
- Fear of having to make decisions you aren't used to making or have never made before.
- Fear of guilt because you are getting over your loss.
- Fear of never getting over the loss.
- Fear of letting your loved one go.
- Fear of not letting your loved one go—what if I can't let go?

- Fear of what others think of you—do they think I'm grieving too much or too little?
- Fear of not being understood while you grieve and even when you're finished grieving.
- Fear of risk.
- Fear of being in the spotlight, of the attention that comes to you when you grieve.
- Fear of liking your new life, which is guilt and a fear of success.
- Fear of not liking your new life.
- Fear of confusion, of being in limbo. In your heart and mind you're not finished with your old life, but you do not have a new one yet.
- When a parent dies, you fear being the elder now and not having your parent to rely on, even when you are an adult. If you're not an adult, you understandably fear being without your parent's support and guidance.

Even when you're doing fine, you still have to deal with other people's fears, which, unfortunately, they may try to instill in you. It's not that they don't want to see you happy, it's that deep down they're jealous because they still haven't gotten over someone, or gotten past their fears, and they resent that you have. As we've all heard before, misery loves company.

In the story of the Golden Calf, in keeping with these human dynamics, the most fearful Israelites passed their fear on to many of their fellow Israelites. After God destroyed the Golden Calf, he killed many of the Israelites. We may safely assume that God killed those very fearful Israelites who had instigated the frenzy, as well as those who eagerly embraced the fear and happily helped create the Golden Calf.

When you are going through something that is life altering, you could lose the friendship of some friends or family. Be prepared for this. People might try to hold you back from healing, because they haven't healed. Do not let them hold you back. Move on past them, too. Let go of them, too. The flip side of this is when people say, "Aren't you over him yet?" They want you to get over your loss quickly, because your pain makes them uncomfortable.

Don't make the same mistakes that the fearful Israelites made. Don't be controlled by your fears, or by anyone else's fears.

Learning from Fear

How does fear teach us? In many surprising ways, often what we fear most can turn out to be something that ends up healing us or opening new doors for us. You can't fear forever. People who can't get past their fears will shut down when they suffer a loss. When this happens, the living become "dead," while the dead remain alive in the grievers' minds.

When you hang on to the reasons behind your fears, you are never going to get anywhere. You won't progress to your "wandering" stage—and healing—because you're afraid to move. You are afraid to move forward, but also afraid to move backward to address those issues at the root of your fears. You're stuck. If you can't move backward first, then you won't be able to move forward.

We all remember times in childhood when we suffered loss, grieved, and were able to move on. When you look back and remember some of those times, they may seem trivial by your adult standards—losing your goldfish when you were six can hardly be compared to losing a husband, wife, parent, or child—but they were pretty important to you then. Still, you grieved and let go. You've been through the process before. We all have a lot of practice at it. We already know how to move forward. We're just overwhelmed by the challenge of moving forward after something so traumatic.

The problem isn't fear—fear is a normal reaction. The problem is we do not know whether we have the power to beat our fear. We don't know if we have the strength to get past it. It's not that we're not supposed to feel fear, it's that we're not supposed to let our natural fears lead us to make poor choices (as in the case of the Israelites when they made the Golden Calf). Those poor choices will stop us from living life the way we should, and they very well may prevent us from healing.

What Are You Really Afraid Of?

We can't say to someone, "Don't be afraid." Fear is a normal part of the process. But we *can* say, "Don't let your fear stop you from doing something, or lead you to do something. Leave fear out of the equation." That means you have to retrain how you think, because we're all very used to basing so much of what we do on fear. The first thing you do when you get into the car is based on fear: you put on your seatbelt. We don't realize just how much of what we do is fear-based, because we're living on automatic pilot.

All of modern society is based upon fear. Ask yourself what's behind nearly everything you say and do and you will realize it's fear. Advertisers want you to be afraid so that you will buy their products and services, which, of course, are supposed to be the answers to all your fears. They want you to worry that you're not "in," not hip, and not impressing your friends and neighbors enough; not thin enough, not pretty enough, not macho enough, and not driving the right car to get dates with supermodels; not safe enough in your home, and not safe enough on the streets; not parenting well enough; not happy enough (gotta buy all those prescription antidepressants you see advertised between dramas!), and not feeling well enough (gotta buy all those prescription drugs you see advertised between the sitcoms!); not getting your clothes white enough or soft enough, not getting the shiniest floor; not looking young enough to compete in the job marketplace (gotta go get that facelift from the local plastic surgeon who advertises in my local paper and on TV!), not making the earth move (gotta go get some Viagra!), not going to keep your husband's affections (gotta go get some Botox for those wrinkles!); and not even going to have a future (better vote for [insert candidate of your choice], or we're all gonna die!). We're already primed to view life through fear-colored glasses. So it is no wonder that we automatically operate from fear whenever we're stressed, particularly when a loved one dies.

Only when you see something (literally or figuratively) can you do something about it. Only when you acknowledge how fear rules our lives can you then take steps to change that. And only when you understand what you're really afraid of—it's not usually what you think it is—can you loosen fear's grip.

What are you really afraid of? The answer may surprise you. Here's an exercise you can do to help you identify your fears:

Step 1: Ask yourself, "What am I afraid of?" or "What are my concerns?"

Step 2: Answer those questions.

Step 3: Ask yourself, "Why?"

Step 4: Answer that.

Step 5: Ask yourself, "Why?"

Step 6: Now answer that.

Step 7: Repeat as many times as you need: Keep peeling back the layers until you get to what's really at the bottom of your fear. Do this with each one of your fears or concerns.

Let's take a look at an example of this exercise in action:

Step 1: What am I afraid of? What are my concerns?

Step 2: Well, I have a number of fears and concerns, but I'll start with this one—I don't feel comfortable going into social settings alone. My husband and I have always shared our life as a couple. Now that he's gone, if I can't get a friend to go with me, I won't even go out to lunch alone.

Step 3: Why?

Step 4: I don't want to sit there alone.

Step 5: Why?

Step 6: Because it feels lonely. I feel uncomfortable. It's not fun. I feel self-conscious.

Step 7: Why?

Step 8: Because people will stare. I might be the only one eating alone in the restaurant.

Step 9: Why is that a problem?

Step 10: Because it makes me feel bad because everyone is sitting with someone, except me. I don't want to stand out or be labeled different because I'm alone. I'll look like some lonely woman who has nobody, who has no friends, who couldn't even find someone to go to lunch with her.

Step 11: Why do you think people would even

pay any attention to whether you're eating alone or not? People are very wrapped up in their own lives. Do you think they're going to take the time to wonder about a stranger sitting alone in a restaurant, to make judgments about you and your life? Why would you think that?

Step 12: Because I'd probably think that if I saw a woman eating alone at a restaurant, I'd think, "What's wrong with her that she has to eat by herself? Doesn't she have any friends? Poor lonely woman."

Step 13: And why would you think that?

Step 14: Because I see being alone as a rejection, as a sign that I'm not worthy, that I'm pathetic, and that others who are alone are not worthy and pathetic, too. If I'm so terrific, why am I alone? Why am I having lunch alone?

Now we're getting somewhere. This woman's concern turned out to be very different than what her first answer implied. Before asking "Why?" after each of her statements, and peeling back the layers, the woman thought that she didn't want to eat alone because it wasn't fun, it was uncomfortable. After peeling away the layers, though, she got to her real, deeper fears and concerns. Only when she deals with those will she be able to enjoy having lunch at a restaurant by herself, and not feel that it's a negative evaluation of her worth as a human being.

For this exercise to work, you have to be willing to be very honest with yourself. The rewards for your honesty, though, are tremendous. You will free yourself from your fears. You will free yourself to have a full life with all the happiness and peace of mind we all deserve.

Turning Fear into Healing and Opportunity

Fears can propel us to take positive, healing actions. Fears can also propel us into wonderful opportunities.

Let's take another look at the woman who was afraid to go out to lunch alone. If you lose your husband, on a simple level you are afraid of being alone. But you can use your fear as a jumping-off point to a new life. Embrace what you fear and make it work for you, not against you.

Are you afraid of being alone? Try to embrace being alone. Look at the situation in a new context. Experience the peacefulness and freedom of spending some time alone (doing what you want, when you want) and being alone with your thoughts. You will learn more about yourself. You'll learn that being alone is not the same as being lonely. You'll learn that it is so much better than surrounding yourself with people, many of whom you may not even like, just to avoid spending some time alone.

When fear no longer holds you back, you will finally be open to new experiences that can enrich your life more than you ever could have imagined. You will meet new people, share new adventures and broaden your horizons—all those clichés you've probably heard other people talk about!

By not letting fear cause you to arbitrarily fill your time with people and activities just to avoid spending time alone, you will be better able to make healthy choices: Who do I really want to spend my time with? Which activities do I want to spend my time doing? What have I been doing and who have I been seeing just to avoid being alone? Who and what should I fill my time with if my goal is to enjoy their company, or the activity, rather than simply avoid being alone? Which activities would I actually enjoy more if I didn't have someone along for company?

Our society discourages people from being self-sufficient. In fact, our entire economy is based on other people doing things for us that we could do for ourselves, including thinking. People are told that their own wisdom is not enough, that they have to turn to the experts in every field imaginable, including the billion-dollar self-help industry. All of this just generates and perpetuates the fear that we can't think for ourselves. We do not trust our own judgment. So we share our problems with others, and those other people often project their fears onto us.

All of this conspires to lead some people to end up worshipping their fears. Does this sound familiar? Although you may not have taken it as far as the Israelites did when their fears and insecurities led them to create and worship a Golden Calf, you may have symbolically done something in the same vein.

Which of your fears have you ended up, in effect, worshipping? Which of your fears have you given power to so
that you answer to the fear, so that you have put accommo-
dating the fear on the top of your to-do list?

As the Israelites awaited Moses's return from his first
trip up to the top of the mountain, they feared they had
lost him, that he would never come back. What were they
really afraid of? Why would the loss of Moses create fear?
Their fears centered on two issues that are common to
many who lose a loved one: *Who am I without him?* and *Who
will take care of me now that he's gone?* Identity and security
fears led the Israelites to seek comfort by creating the
Golden Calf to worship.

Have identity and security fears led you to worship anything material? Or any activity? Have you "drowned your
sorrows" in alcohol, drugs, food, shopping, sex, gambling,
or any other potentially addictive pursuits? Have you sought
comfort in anything or anyone else that is ultimately not
good for you?

Or have you gone in the opposite direction and become
reclusive and emotionally paralyzed by your grief, fears,
and identity and security issues? Have you used your fears
as reasons for not doing something, or for doing something? Is fear usually in the equation somewhere, no matter
what you do or do not do? Healing can't begin until you
begin to leave fear out of the equation.

You can look at loss from a negative standpoint, a neutral one, or a positive one. Loss, in and of itself, is nothing.
It is all in how you respond to it. Loss just is. You'll be

reminded of that a lot in this book. You give loss meaning by how you respond to it. If you respond with fear, then loss will be fearful. If your response is discovery of a new life and new possibilities, then that is the kind of experience you will have. You can view loss as either closing a door or opening one. Closing is fear-based, opening is not.

Loss can lead you to positive, creative directions if you do not succumb to the kind of fearful thinking that is represented by the unfortunate old saying, "It's a choice between the devil you know versus the devil you don't know." New experiences aren't necessarily other devils, and in fact they usually aren't. They're quite often angels, great experiences. So don't stay in unfulfilling or bad situations out of fear.

We can learn a lot from a story told by Rabbi Dov Peretz Elkins, in his book *Moments of Transcendence* (Northvale, NJ : J. Aronson, 1992), about how one of God's creatures reacted when the world, quite literally, dumped on him:

> One day, a farmer's donkey fell down into a well. The animal cried piteously for hours as the farmer tried to figure out what to do. Finally, he decided the animal was old, and the well needed to be covered up anyway; it just wasn't worth it to retrieve the donkey. He invited all his neighbors to come over and help him. They all grabbed a shovel and began to shovel dirt into the well.
>
> At first, the donkey realized what was happening and cried horribly. Then, to everyone's amazement, he quieted down. A few shovel loads later, the farmer

finally looked down the well. He was astonished at what he saw. With each shovel of dirt that hit his back, the donkey was doing something amazing. He would shake it off and take a step up. As the farmer's neighbors continued to shovel dirt on top of the animal, he would shake it off and take a step up. Pretty soon, everyone was amazed as the donkey stepped up over the edge of the well and happily trotted off!

As Rabbi Elkins reminds us, "The trick to getting out of the well is to have hope; to shake off the dirt and take a step up, and realize that if we do not give up, we can get out of even the deepest well." Had the donkey operated out of fear, he probably would've stood there and let the dirt fall until it buried—and killed—him. How will you react when the world shovels dirt on you? When it hands you loss, pain, and grief?

Most people look at the world as *either/or*. Look at it, instead, as *both/and:* you can see loss as both an end and a beginning. People are just as afraid of beginnings as they are of loss, because they're afraid of the unknown, but usually they assume the unknown must be something awful out there waiting for them instead of something great.

When you lose someone and you're grieving, you feel vulnerable. That feeling of vulnerability heightens fears you may already have and creates new ones. When you let go of all of those fears, you can transform the "losing" into a "finding" as you find a healthy, new, fear-free life.

Turning Fear into Opportunity

Take a look at your fears, one by one, and with each one ask yourself, "What's the worst that can happen?" Then ask yourself how you can turn that into an opportunity.

A woman whose husband died feared losing her home, because, financially, the upkeep was too much for her. She had become, in effect, a financial prisoner of her home. Everything she did and did not do was based on the financial burden placed upon her by her house. But what she feared most would actually be the answer to all of her problems: if she no longer had the house, her stress level would plummet, and her life would improve dramatically.

One day it occurred to her that instead of living in fear that she would lose her house, she should just put it on the market and sell it, buy a smaller, more affordable place to live, and end up with enough money to maintain her new home and enjoy her life. She turned her fear into opportunity. She is no longer stressed by her situation, and she is now financially and emotionally comfortable.

So it is possible for us to overcome our fears and even to transform them into healing memories. When we move past a fear, it will no longer paralyze us; instead, it will remind us how far we've come in our grief journey. The fear will fade, the memory will retreat, but the hope will remain.

No matter what we fear, we can learn from and take comfort from what Nelson Mandela said in his inaugural address as president of South Africa:

Our deepest fear is not that we are inadequate. Our deepest fear is that we are powerful beyond measure. It is our light, not our darkness that most frightens us. We ask ourselves: Who am I to be brilliant, gorgeous, talented and fabulous? Actually, who are you not to be? You are a child of God. Your playing small doesn't serve the world. There is nothing enlightened about shrinking so that other people won't feel insecure around you. We were born to make manifest the glory of God that is within us. It's not just in some of us; it's in everyone. And as we let our own light shine, we unconsciously give other people permission to do the same. As we are liberated from our own fear, our presence automatically liberates others.

CHAPTER 7

Wandering and Healing

The Story: The Israelites Wander in the Desert for Forty Years, from the Book of Numbers

⁓

WHEN SOMEONE DIES, our lives are forever altered. We know this in our heads, but in our hearts we wish for the same certainty that we had before they died. We want everything to be the same, but it never will be again. And so begins our period of wandering—from who we are now to who we will become at the end of our grief journey.

After Moses led the Israelites out of Egypt, where they had been slaves, they wandered in the desert for forty years before God would let them into the Promised Land. God only wanted those who had been born free, who would never know slavery, to enter Israel. Those who had been slaves had to die out before their descendants would be allowed to enter the Promised Land.

After the loss of a loved one, which is essentially the loss of a way of life, the "old you" can't enter its new life until it "dies" and is replaced by the "new you." This process is a form of wandering, and you must go through that phase of grief recovery before you arrive at hope and your future.

When you're wandering, you are really wandering in two directions at the same time. Part of you wants to go back, and part of you wants to go forward. That was also true of the Israelites when they were wandering in the desert with Moses. They did not want to go back to being slaves, of course, but they did want to go back to the familiarity of home in Egypt. It was predictable and known, and they were afraid, like everyone is, of the unknown.

By letting them wander for forty years in the desert, God would be assured not only that no one who had known slavery would enter the Promised Land, but also that the only people who would enter Israel were those who had been born in the desert and did not think of Egypt as home.

They were free of any conflict regarding "home." They did not miss Egypt, because they had never lived there, and they didn't feel a pull to some other place. The desert was the only place they knew. They were a clean slate, ready to enter the Promised Land. Of course, that never happens with grief. Your mind is never a clean slate. You will always have your memories, and it's those pangs of memory that cause grief. But you can be healed before entering the Promised Land. Wandering is that early phase of healing, after shock, anger, and fear, when you begin to sort things out. During your wandering, your memories pull you backward, and your unknown future—without the person you are mourning—pulls you forward.

Wandering is wondering. You wonder what your new life will look like, how you will go on without the person you have lost.

Wandering is also wanting. You want the loss never to have happened, you want your loved one back. You want the pain to end, you want to know that you'll be okay, and you want to know that the future has promise . . . your own version of entering into the Promised Land.

When will your healing truly begin? It will begin when you want to go forward more than you want to go backward. When the future becomes appealing, and you are not just focusing on the past, even though the future has unknowns and the past is familiar. When you think of your past as just a part of you instead of the entire you. When your past is integrated into you and gives you wisdom to bring it with you into the future. When you realize that you are not leaving your past behind, but are taking it inside you and integrating it into your whole being and heart. You now realize that the past is no longer where you see your future. Instead, you see a new future, one whose unknowns are possibilities and nothing to be afraid of.

Grief recovery is all about integration: integrating your past into your life in a way that allows you to go healed into the future.

Leaving the Desert: Robert at Terminal 2

Like the Israelites born in the desert during that forty-year journey, some people are born wandering. Unfortunately, quite a number of them become casualties of that wandering, because they have never had hope and could never even imagine a Promised Land. They die along their way to nowhere.

But others who were born wandering do allow themselves to have hope; they're not afraid to feel hopeful, and they can envision a future. They do not believe that their wandering past and present must define the rest of their lives.

Robert is one such man. I met Robert back in June 2001, when I was wandering around Newark International Airport with six hours to kill before my flight. I bought a book and sat down by my departure gate to read. Every few chapters I would get up and walk around the terminal. After about two hours, I got really antsy, so I took a long ride around the monorail that circles the airport. I got off at Terminal 2. That wasn't my terminal, but I was on an adventure, such as it was, and thought I'd look around. I took the elevator down to the boarding level. It was then that I first saw—or, rather, heard—Robert.

A robust tenor voice filled the place with song. Why was someone singing in the middle of the airport? Whoever he was, I though he sounded a lot like Robert Goulet. Had I stumbled upon some Broadway musical performer? I followed the sound of this magnificent voice, and it led me to a man in his fifties, dressed in an airport uniform. He looked like Geoffrey Holder, the Tony Award—winning actor who also carved a place in our collective pop culture memory on the famous TV commercials for 7-up, where his deep, soothing voice exhaled in an island accent: "The Un-Cola."

But Robert was not a Tony Award–winning Broadway actor; he was an airport employee whose job it was to direct passengers to their gates, the ticket counter, the food court, or wherever else they needed to go. He sang out greetings to passengers—not just in English, but in many other languages as well. He sang out answers to passengers' questions. He sang out directions. Anytime someone asked him for directions—or for any other assistance—with great gusto he answered in song. This brought huge smiles to the faces of everyone who spoke to him, and everyone within earshot.

What a nice way to spend your day, I thought, *to see your job as an opportunity for not only your own creative self-expression, but to make other people happy. What could be better than that?* And it reminded me that that is one of the reasons I like my job so much—I get to do the same thing.

I listened for a while, realizing that I, too, was smiling, and then I left. I went back up the elevator, got back on the monorail, and went back to my own terminal, where I once again parked myself on one of those plastic airport chairs and read.

About a half hour later, I looked up, and to my surprise, I spotted Robert walking along in my terminal, walking along my concourse. I figured he was probably on a break. My curiosity was piqued, so I walked up to him, introduced myself, and invited him to tell me his story.

He told me that he'd been raised in a poor, small town in Georgia. "There was no hope in that town," he said.

Everybody left and nobody came back. I felt like I had no hope, either. I got in lots of trouble as a kid, because there was nothing else to do. I even spent some time in jail. Then I got out and took a job. I was going nowhere when my mama told me that I had a gift. I asked her what she thought that gift was. And she said it was my beautiful voice. She said that anybody with a voice like mine ought to use it to do God's work. I just laughed at her and give her a big kiss, and forgot all about it.

The next Sunday, we all went to church, like we did every Sunday. The preacher was reading from the book of Psalms, and he came to Psalm 86, verse 16: "Happy is the people who know Thy joyful shout, O Lord, they walk in the light of Your Presence." Something holy happened to me at that moment. I didn't know what it was then, but now I know it was God talking to me personally. I couldn't stop shaking in church, and I figured, "That is it! Now I know what I have to do." I listened to God and my mama, and I applied for a job with the airlines. The rest is history. I've been doing this job for more than twenty years, and I still love making people happy. Airports can be horrible places to spend time, and there are lots of unhappy people here. I try to make them happy.

And now I was one of the people infused with Robert's joy. I had started out the day bored and annoyed by having to kill hours and hours at the airport, but now I was energized.

I was blown away by his poignant story, his magnificent voice, and his undiluted joy in his life's work.

I believe that nothing happens to us by accident. I believe that we are somehow meant to meet the people we meet when we meet them. They come to us for a reason: to teach us a specific lesson. We may not know at that particular time why they come into our lives, and we may not immediately know what the lesson is—it may hit us later—but at some point it always becomes clear to us.

All I know is that Robert at Terminal 2 changed my life that day. Meeting him taught me many lessons and reminded me of others I'd forgotten in the busy, crazy, swirl of life. Much later, as I thought about the kinds of wandering people do, I remembered Robert's story and realized that I had met someone who exemplified hope, someone who had been born wandering, but who grabbed on to that hope when it presented itself in the form of his mother's words and his preacher's reciting of an inspiring psalm that spoke directly to him.

Nearly thirty years ago now, Robert left his wandering in the desert and entered his Promised Land. All it took was hope, faith, and courage. He recognized hope when it presented itself. He had faith in the meaning behind the divine coincidence that brought to him the on-target words of that psalm right after hearing the encouraging words of his mother. He was not afraid to leave the desert. He was not afraid to stop wandering. He was not afraid to envision a better future. He did not continue wandering, as so many other people do, out of the fear that he might be disappointed by taking chances on a future.

How Healing Takes You Back to the Future

When you are grieving, the goal of healing is not to get you back to where you were before you suffered the loss. That is not good enough. The goal of healing is to get you back to the future, to get you into a position where you will be better able to deal with the grief you'll feel from your next loss. The goal is to make you stronger, wiser, and more emotionally equipped to go through the grief recovery process the next time. And there *will* be a next time. Life has ups and downs, gains and losses. That doesn't stop as long as you are alive.

You are a partner in healing with your body and mind. You are an active participant in the healing process. If you don't help your body and mind, it's the same as working against them. The body is a gift from God, but there's "some assembly required." The mind, heart, spirit, and body are all wired for healing, but they need our assistance. One of our Jewish prayers says, "Thank you, God, who has created the human body with wisdom."

So much of our emotional healing takes place on the subconscious level. Even our dreams help us heal, by giving us clues and stories that point to some of the areas that still need to heal. I spoke with a woman who has always had very vivid dreams and had experienced a series of what she called "closure dreams" about a loved one she had lost, not through death, but through a relationship breakup. For a number of years after the breakup, she would have one or two of these dreams a year, in which she and her former beloved had the kind of forgiveness and closure conversations they'd never had when they broke up or afterward. Her subconscious was working all this out through dream scenarios that gradually contributed to her healing, her grief recovery process. Years after she had felt healed, she still had at least one of these dreams every year, as if to reinforce the lessons she had learned from the relationship.

In her book *Final Passage: Sharing the Journey as This Life Ends* (Deerfield Beach, FL: Health Communications, 1998), death and dying researcher and counselor Barbara Harris Whitfield wrote about the emotional, psychological, spiritual, and physical aspects of peoples' dying processes and grief experiences. She also wrote about her own experiences with the death of her parents, with whom she'd had challenging relationships. First, her father died, and then a year and a month later, her mother died. Already well into her career in counseling others, now it was Barbara's turn to deal with grief issues. "After each of my parents died, I went around and around feeling my pain, letting it go and feeling it again," she wrote. "Grieving is a strange state."

After her mother died, Barbara had a dream in which she saw both of her parents' souls and had a conversation with her mother's. Her mother didn't know where she and her husband were, so Barbara told her that they were dead. Barbara's mother then asked what she and Barbara's father were supposed to do. When Barbara told her they could go be with God, her mother said they didn't know how to do that.

"Follow my prayers," Barbara said. Then she prayed that God would receive her parents. She watched her parents float away. As they moved with her prayers, Barbara felt a sharp pain exiting her body, out of her back at her heart's level.

In the dream she thought, "I know a part of me has gone with them. I know they are with God. I feel at peace, and I am happy for them." In the dream they weren't the difficult people they had been in life. Instead, they were pure souls, and this, too, helped Barbara. "My grieving process has lightened up since that dream," Barbara wrote. "I sense that most of my pain over my parents' deaths is over. Occasionally, I still grieve for them, for me and for what we missed."

Barbara's insights about the grief recovery process have been deepened by her own experiences. "And through all of this grief work, I have learned to let go of trying to control this process. Like my mother in my dream, I am disarmed. I have no defensiveness left against feeling my feelings. I have experientially learned from the loss of my father and my mother that we can't control grieving . . . It comes and it goes," she wrote. "But when it flares up—watch out. Listen to it, to its needs. We need to stop doing and just be with it. The more we struggle against it or try to ignore it, the greater the flare-up becomes. This process of grief is a caving in and a letting go and a breaking through to feelings."

Your spirit helps your mind heal your heart. With your mind you understand what you have to do to heal, but you heal *from* the heart and *for* the heart. Your heart is broken, your mind is not. But if you do not heal, not only will you continue to have a broken heart, but your mind will break as well. And your spirit will, too. We've all heard the phrase, "his spirit was broken."

Even when you're not thinking about your grief or healing, your mind is working on the subconscious level—with the aid of your body and spirit—to continue the healing process. Your mind takes in everything during the day and processes some of it toward healing even when you are not consciously thinking about it. Something you see, do, or hear, something you read, something someone says or does, contributes to your healing.

In the same way a cast protects a broken leg, you can protect your broken heart while it heals. When you think about it, we're always grieving something or someone to one degree or another. We heal from one loss while we're still working on healing from another. We experience new losses before we've fully recovered from the old ones. If we're not in denial and are honest with ourselves, we probably spend more time mourning our disappointments and the loss of our illusions than anything, or anyone, else. It's best to take the time to properly note and mourn them. If we do not, we risk becoming angry, bitter, resentful, and pessimistic, and wallowing in self-pity far more often than it's ever healthy for anyone to wallow.

In Job 14:7 we're reminded, "There is hope for a tree; if it is cut down it will renew itself; its shoots will not cease." And neither will yours. But, like a tree's renewal, your renewal does not happen instantly.

We do not have some drive-through place called "Grieve 'n' Go"; grief recovery takes time. During that time, be open and honest with yourself and with others. Seek the truth from others. When people do not get the truth, they can't heal. That is why people want closure so much—closure is the truth.

Terri Schiavo, Dead and Still Alive

Let's talk about the long, drawn-out saga of Terry Schiavo, since her death illustrates many aspects of wandering. Who among us was not moved by the drama of her extended illness, especially her last days? I know I was. Her death was not the way I would want my own death to be. When my time comes, I want no heroic measures, since for me they simply postpone the inevitable. And watching the family feud that took place between Terry's husband and her parents, with all the tension and the anger, saddened me terribly. Peace should be the last emotion Terry felt, but who knows if she heard only the angry words passed between those she loved? No one should have to die as she did. What a shame.

At the same time, look at the two different approaches to grief presented to us, one by her husband, Michael, and the other by her parents, Robert and Mary Schindler. Michael was clearly ready to "lay her gently down"; he was prepared to move on with his new life and to "begin again" with his fiancée and their two young children. Some say he was ready a bit too soon, but I disagree. Grief takes only as long as it needs, and no longer. Michael had wandered for years in his own desert of loneliness, and now he was clearly ready for a new life. Her parents, on the other hand, were unable to give her up yet. For them, the wandering had not yet begun. It is understandable that parents would be so protective of their children, and I don't know what I would do if, God forbid, one of my own kids was in a similar state.

I am not judging, but rather pointing out the differences in style and approach in this wrenching drama. For Terri's parents, despite how they may have felt then, I hope they know there is still hope for them. There is a new future that they will soon help create; there will be new challenges for them and their family that they cannot yet know. When you are grieving, you often lose sight of the future, because the present is so draining. But no matter what has been taken from you, there is hope.

The Schindlers still have each other and they still have a life in front of them. I certainly pray that they will find healing and consolation, and that Terri's memories will bring them peace.

Life Can Go On

I remember many years ago I had a congregant family whose college-age daughter was dying of a rare disease. The end came slowly, so her parents and I had lots of time to talk about life and death and God's place in all this sadness. *Is there a God? Why is God doing this to us? How can we go on without our daughter?* We discussed these and similar theological questions day and night. One morning the doctor examined her and told us that the end was near. The girl's father turned to me and said, "We want to donate her organs so that someone else can live through her." I went and notified the proper transplant staff, and when I returned to the hospital room, I asked the father, "Did your decision have anything to do with the questions about God that we have been having?" He turned to me with tears in his eyes and said, "I still don't know right now what I think about God, but I do know that when these organs are transplanted, there will be another mom and dad who won't have to ask about whether or not there is a God, because they will be so grateful for the gift of life they have received. And whether I believe in him or not, I guess that is really what God wants me to do, isn't it?" From sadness came hope. And I'm sure God was smiling.

What's Your Leaving Style?

Each of us has our own "leaving style," our own way of saying good-bye, and that style stays with us for our entire lives. No one knows why we each have different leaving styles.

If you want to know what your leaving style is, here's a sure-fire way of discovering it. Think of the last party you went to. When it was time for you to leave, how did you say good-bye? Some people leave quickly, without saying good-bye to everyone. In fact, some of us do not even say good-bye to our hosts, we just leave. Some of us leave in the exact opposite way; we walk around and say good-bye to everyone there, and then (sometimes hours later!) we finally leave. Some of us leave without saying good-bye, and some say good-bye but don't leave!

The way you leave a party will be the exact same way you will leave other parts of your life. It is your leaving style, and it's very hard to change it, even if you want to. For example, most of us grew up believing that once we made a friend, that friendship would last forever. Of course, some friendships do last forever, and they are a blessing to us and to our friends. But what happens when it's time for a friendship to end, when it's time to say good-bye? Sometimes we move away, or our friends move away, and we just lose touch with each other. We all know how hard it is to sustain friendships, even under the best of circumstances. But sometimes something bad or sad happens, and we realize that the friendship we had thought would last forever is over, because it just can't be saved. Perhaps we've been hurt by our (former) friend, perhaps we've grown differently and have less and less in common with them. Whatever the reason, the friendship no longer works, and it is time to end it. How will we do that?

Once again, our own leaving styles take over. Some of us will end our friendships with honor and dignity; we will say good-bye and thank our friends for the joy that they gave to us, even as we begin emotionally to disconnect. Some of us will just disappear, or be abrupt and say nothing, or we might even get angry with a former friend as a pretext for ending the friendship. For some of us, that is easier than being honest with them, and with ourselves, about what's really going on in our heads and in our hearts. We also end romantic relationships in a way that is consistent with our leaving style.

You've probably figured out where this is heading. When our time comes to leave this world, once again our leaving styles show themselves. You may know people whose lives are coming to an end, and who make time to say good-bye to those who meant something to them. They will begin to wrap things up, to apologize to whomever they have hurt, to forgive those who have hurt them, and to repair those relationships that have come undone. As someone recently said to me two days before she died, "Rabbi, I need to do this before I get to the other side." We all know what she means.

But you also know others who just leave this world without expressing any gratitude to those who have shared life with them, or any remorse for those words and deeds that had brought pain to others.

It's just like at a party; some say good-bye and take a long time to leave, and some just leave without saying good-bye. The way you leave a party is the way you will leave "the final party" of life.

What's your leaving style? What have been the leaving styles of those you lost, whether to death or relationship breakup? Their leaving styles will greatly affect your grief experience and recovery. Do you have loose ends or the potential for closure?

The Real-Life Wandering Jew

Your wandering will take you through all of the aspects of grief recovery you'll find in this book. You will be wandering for a while, and that is as it should be. Wandering is a process, and so is healing. Neither one is accomplished overnight.

Any botanist will tell you that the wandering Jew is a unique plant that—even when given minimal substance—will nevertheless spread and grow. If you cut its roots off and plant it rootless in other soil, it will regenerate itself and start anew. The griever is like this wandering Jew plant: feeling rootless, not knowing where to go, perhaps not really wanting to go in any particular direction. Sometimes the griever wants to remain in place and grow new roots, not moving for fear of having to make decisions and not having any idea how to do that.

Like everyone else, I've done my share of wandering. When my mother died almost thirty years ago, I was in my late twenties, and I began my wandering by not wanting to move at all. When I returned from the cemetery, I felt like a dishrag that had been used and discarded. I was physically and emotionally exhausted from the funeral and just wanted to escape into my bedroom, tuck myself into the safety of my bed and under my blanket, and never, ever, come out of my room again.

I was not interested in being comforted by anyone, I didn't care if I ever ate again, I didn't care about anything. I was truly beginning my trek through the desert. Where would I end up? What would happen to me? At that particular time in my life, when my mother, the most important person in my life, had just died, I really didn't care very much what happened to me. I just wanted to be left alone. I was a zombie, spacewalking through life without much passion. My mother had died, and part of my life had died with her.

So how did I finally get better? How did I manage to wander through my grief desert and come out whole on the other side? Several factors saved me from remaining in that desert. First, there was life itself. I knew that I had to get up every morning, get out of bed, and function as an adult. People counted on me. I was needed, and being needed helped me to move forward through the desert of my wandering.

Some people say the secret to happiness can be broken down into three elements: something to do, someone to love, and something to look forward to. I had something to do—I was a rabbi, and my congregants were counting on me to function for them as I had before. In part, they were observing how I made my way through my wandering, because they, too, had been wounded by life's losses and they needed to see how I navigated mine.

I also had someone to love. In fact, I had lots of someones to love. I had my wife, and others whom I loved who loved me, too. Members of my family and my friends supported me and gave me the community that I so desperately needed. I was not the kind of person who would do well grieving with a lot of alone time.

Finally, I had something to look forward to: my wife and I were expecting our first child. There's nothing like anticipating a joyous event to bring out our life forces. We are wired to get energetic when we anticipate something, and I was.

When joy meets sadness, joy must win out. We need to focus on the upcoming celebration, and when we do, the sadness will begin to recede. Yes, I was sad that my mother had died and that she wouldn't be with me to meet her first grandchild, but I knew that she would be there with me in spirit, and that I would be sharing our child's birth with her. This helped anchor me to life at a time when I really did not feel like participating in the world.

How to Wander

There is no GPS for wandering. No map, and no direct route. You try out things, you meander, you experiment and see what works for you and what doesn't. You go through your wandering step by step, not all at once. You think, you evaluate, you mourn, you learn, you let go of things, you create, you heal.

What can you think and do during your wandering that will help you heal and recover from grief? Here are some ideas you might want to keep in mind:

> 1. Don't have a predetermined idea of who you're going to be at the end of your wandering. Be free while you wander, be open, and leave

room for serendipity. Who you'll be when you finish wandering is much different than what you might have predicted. What happens during your wandering will contribute to who you'll be at the end, and you can't know about any of that ahead of time.

2. Remember that wandering is called *wandering* for a reason: it *is* wandering. You're supposed to be wandering—or to paraphrase *Merriam-Webster's Collegiate Dictionary,* moving about without a fixed course, aim, or goal—not knowing where you will end up. Just know from the beginning that however you wander, wherever you wander emotionally (or even geographically), when you are finished, you'll be okay.

3. Every person finds their own way while they're wandering. Your wandering won't look like anybody else's. And neither will your grief or your healing.

4. Along the way, you will be tempted to ask yourself (or God), "Are we there yet?" You may believe you're finished wandering, only to begin wandering again soon, or even much later. This is perfectly normal. Eventually, you will know that you're finished with the major part of your grief wandering. When you don't have to ask yourself if you're finished. You'll sense it, and you will know that your grief

wandering is over. Do not worry if you have mini-wanderings after you feel done, that is normal. We all wander a little, all the time, and that contributes to our growth and well-being.

5. Your wandering may feel aimless, but it does have a purpose and an ultimate destination. You don't have to know where that is yet. You'll recognize it when you get there. The purpose of wandering is to heal, grow, and become the new you. This process has its ups and downs, its good days and bad days, its good moments and bad moments, its good weeks and bad weeks. You may feel like you're progressing really well, and then feel like you're backsliding. This is normal, it's part of the process. Just go with it.

6. There are different ways to wander. You can do it focusing on yourself sometimes, and you can do it looking outside yourself as an observer at other times. As an observer, you'll be reflective, and you won't get too bogged down by what happens to you at the time. If you are feeling down one day, you will just go with the feeling, realize it's okay, and not be hard on yourself.

7. Remember that wandering is a gradual process. You get a little bit better as you go along. You don't wander in one day or get

better in one day. There's an old Hasidic saying: "There's no clock for the soul." Wandering will take as long as it takes. Healing will take as long as it takes. It may take less time than you thought it would, or it may take more time than you thought it would. It might even take about the same time you thought it would. There is no proper amount of time, and there is no schedule for the healing journey of wandering. Do not listen to anyone who says that you are healing too quickly or healing too slowly.

8. When you're grieving, you often lose sight of the future, because the present is so draining. This happens from the moment grief begins and continues to some degree while you are wandering. As you feel less drained, you will be more able to envision a future.

9. As you wander, remember that everyone you meet is also wandering. They may be grieving someone or something, or they may be in a wandering phase because of a major life change. They may be spiritually or philosophically wandering. The bottom line is that everyone is wandering to some degree, all the time, even you, even when you're not in the midst of a major grief experience. When you've recovered and healed from your grief, you will still do a bit of wandering from time

to time for other reasons. You may not have thought of this process as wandering. You may be more familiar with its other name: *life*.

10. Knowing that everyone, including you, is always wandering to some degree, may give you some compassion for yourself and others. Go easy on yourself while you are wandering. Go easy on everyone else while they're wandering.

11. During the grief process, you may do some literal wandering: you may move from your old home to a new one, from your city to another one. You may stay with family or friends for a while, and then go back to your home or to a new home.

12. Remember that wandering is that period of time when you feel lost, when you feel like you're just "wandering in your own life," when your emotions are up and down, when you're wondering about everything, when you feel like you're just going through the motions, when you're wondering what in the world to do with yourself now that you've lost your loved one, or been through another kind of loss. You'll wonder how to live without who or what you lost, you'll wonder if you can make it day by day. You'll wonder what your future will look like. You'll wonder why you feel the way you feel. You'll be a human question

mark. And you may be unsure about what you're "supposed" to think or not think. All of this is normal.

13. Go with the flow; do not hide your feelings from yourself, and don't slip into denial. Do not try to hold it all in. Feel what you're feeling, and ride it out. You won't always feel this bad. Believe it or not, you will feel better. While you wander, talk with people who understand you, and avoid sharing your feelings with those who do not.

14. While you wander, it is normal for you to feel better for a while and then feel worse when something triggers a sharp emotional pain. The pain will recede again. This will happen even after you've completed the major part of your wandering. Think about a man with a broken arm. The worst pain comes at the moment of injury and immediately after. The pain recedes after a week or so, and then gradually gets better. About six weeks after the injury, the cast comes off. He's feeling much better, but the arm still feels a bit tender now that it is not protected by the cast. A few months later, it is as if nothing ever happened. His arm is fine. But something strange happens when the weather changes. When the pressure drops, the humidity rises, and it is about to rain, his arm

aches. Weather triggers the pain in the old wound of a broken, but now healed, bone. You will find that a wide variety of "internal weather" very specific to you, your life, and your memories, will trigger the pain in the old wound of your broken, but now healed, heart. Just as the aching arm will feel better shortly when the bout of bad weather is over, your aching heart will also feel better when the effects of your trigger wear off.

Myths about Grief

While you are wandering through grief recovery, you will likely hear some of the unfortunate and useless comments that our society believes helps those who are in mourning get over their loss. I'm not entirely convinced that most people who offer such comments are ignorant enough to actually believe their words help. I think that some people who offer what they believe is consolation hope their words help, even though they suspect that they do not. And I think that others buy into these myths and offer them up to grievers for lack of anything else to say. Either way, the important thing to remember is: many of these comments won't help you in any way. When you hear them, just ignore them, and try to resist getting into a debate about them with whomever offered. Do not waste your precious emotional energy. Just smile, nod, and ignore it all.

When I was ready to learn about grief and hope, I turned to the Grief Recovery Institute in Los Angeles, a well-known and well-respected institution. They taught me what they knew about grief, loss, and hope; they supported me in my mission to assist those in pain; and they invited me to grow my gifts and talents in this area. In short, they became my "grief rabbis." The Grief Recovery Institute highlights some of the worst of society's responses to grief:

"Don't feel bad."

You've gotta be kidding. Of course you are going to feel bad, and you should. It is only natural, healthy, and emotionally honest to feel bad when you've suffered a painful loss. The only way you are going to heal is to feel bad first. If you suppress your true feelings, you will never recover. "Don't feel bad" is usually followed by another comment tailored to the situation:

- Divorce or relationship breakup: "He was a jerk and you are better off without him, or "She was never good enough for you anyway."
- Miscarriage: "This baby wasn't meant to be born."
- Any death: "God needed him/her more than you did."

"We'll get you another one."

When your first pet died, what did Mom or Dad say? "Don't worry, we'll get you another one." But you didn't want another one—you wanted the one you had! When you lose a relationship to death or breakup, other, well-meaning people may think you need an immediate replacement. This is not much different from Mom and Dad's response to your poor, departed pet.

Here's another example, just for women: do you remember when you were in eighth grade, and your boyfriend, the absolute love of your life, broke up with you for the cute redheaded cheerleader who sat in the third row in English class, and how you cried and cried all night long after it happened? Your parents probably said something like: "Don't worry, there are lots more fish in the sea!" But you didn't want *another* fish, you wanted *that* one!

"Stop crying!"

"Why bother crying? It won't do you any good," or "Go to your room if you want to cry." These are two typical comments made to young grievers, and even to adult grievers by older adults. If you hear this comment as a child while you're grieving a death, you'll grow up thinking you're supposed to keep your feelings to yourself and that no one is interested in how you feel or in comforting you. No matter what your age, you'll also interpret such words as meaning it is best not to speak about death or the feelings that are associated with it.

"Just give it time."

While time does help us heal, time all by itself will not help. It's what we do during that time that can help us heal.

Thinking that time is all you need will lead you to erroneously believe that you do not have to do anything about grief, that time will take care of everything. This is as helpful as saying if you fall down the stairs and break your arm, you don't have to do anything about it—just wait and time will heal your arm. A broken heart hurts just as much as a broken arm, and must be tended to as soon as possible. Many of us know people who are still mourning a loved one who died twenty years ago, a mourner who is still waiting for "time to heal."

Time is neutral. It only heals if we engage in healing actions. Time by itself just passes.

"Be strong for [insert name of relative or other lost loved one]."

I can still hear my uncle saying to me right after I'd been told that my father had died, "Melvin, you have to be the man of the house now." First of all, I hardly ever saw my father during the week. He worked every day except Sunday, so I had absolutely no idea what the "man of the house" did. And, second, I was all of twelve years old. I was not a man, and didn't want to be one yet.

We all need to be needed, to feel as if our lives matter, especially after someone whose life mattered to us has died. But to tell us to be strong for others without allowing us to "be weak for ourselves" just doesn't work. No one should tell us to be strong for someone we've lost, no matter how old the mourner is.

"Keep busy."

Mourners are often told to keep busy so that they do not have time to dwell on their feelings. This faulty advice is meant to protect us from our pain, but it never works. It just encourages us to hide from reality, to pretend that nothing is wrong. We all know from experience what happens if we hide from our feelings: it only postpones the inevitable confrontation with grief that we so desperately need in order to heal our hearts. The longer you hide from your feelings, the more painful it will be when they finally explode out of their cave.

Wandering through Unresolved Grief

In *The Grief Recovery Handbook* authors John W. James and Russell Friedman offer signs that let you know that you need help with your grief:

1. When you're unwilling to talk about someone who has died.
2. When fond memories turn painful, so that when you mention your deceased loved one's name, it's as if a dagger goes through your heart.
3. When you can talk only about your loved one's positive aspects (enthronement), or only about their negative aspects (bedevilment), you're creating an incomplete portrait. Ask yourself why.

4. When subsequent relationships are difficult,
   and when you go through one boyfriend or
   spouse after another, you have unresolved
   grief, signaling that you're having difficulty
   "completing your relationship" with the one
   who has died.

Grief Recovery Loss History

During our wandering, our grief recovery process, one of
our goals is to "complete the relationship" with those
we've lost. Created by the Grief Recovery Institute, the
healing exercise below can be valuable in determining
which relationships we haven't completed, and then to
helping us to complete them. And, yes, we can complete
relationships with those who are no longer in our lives as
well as those who are no longer living.

1. Write down all the losses that you can
   remember—people living or dead, as well as
   the situations surrounding these losses.
2. With each loss, write down all the bad advice
   that you received regarding that particular loss.
3. With each loss, write down all the not-so-
   healthy actions that you thought would help
   you cope, such as eating too much or too little,
   drinking too much or using drugs, shopping
   too much, making important life decisions in
   haste, entering a romantic relationship on the
   rebound, repressing your feelings, pretending

you didn't care, and anything else you can remember.

4. Reflect on everything included in your loss history lists, and determine which former relationship is the most incomplete. Later, you can also single out other relationships that are incomplete.

When I did this loss history exercise, I discovered that my most incomplete relationship was with my mother. She had been dead for many years, but our relationship had never been completed.

I had many feelings about the loss of my mother—after all, that is what grief is, the normal and natural feelings one has after a loss. It helped me a lot to write down the particular losses in my life. Finally, I had "put a voice" to them. Now I could reflect on them and the feelings they had caused.

At first I tried to make light of these losses, wondering whether or not they all truly qualified as losses. That was when I realized the Institute's First Truth of grief recovery: *If they feel like losses, then they are losses.* The Second Truth followed: *Every loss is mourned at 100 percent.* There are no "minor losses." Each loss matters to us, from a spouse's death to a best friend moving away, from a romantic breakup or divorce to the loss of a pet, from a job loss to the loss of an illusion.   Listing my life losses gave me the opportunity to grieve them, some for the first time. I was focused, and I could not ignore or escape my losses. They were mine and I needed to "own them." Writing them down brought them out of the shadows and gave them meaning.

As I filled out my loss history, my true emotions could finally surface, and all of these emotions helped me to be able to say good-bye to my mother, to complete my relationship with her, so many years after her death.

Letter of Release

The next exercise in the process is writing a letter of release. When I wrote mine to my mother, I accomplished several goals:

- I thanked her for all the good that she had given me in our relationship.
- I forgave her for the pain she had caused me.
- I apologized to her for the pain I had caused her.
- Finally, I said good-bye.

I read my two-page letter to a close, supportive friend. This is one of the keys to forgiveness: hearing your own words said out loud so you will own them. Do not read your letter to the person you are saying good-bye to if he or she is alive. If my mother had been alive, I would not have read this letter to her, because the issue of forgiveness was mine, not hers. I was the one carrying the pain of our relationship, so I was the one who had to do the grief work necessary to bring me healing. Reading such a letter to the object of our grief accomplishes nothing, and it only exacerbates the conflict. I imagined what my mother might have said upon hearing such a letter: "What do you mean I caused you pain? It was your own fault for not listening to me."

I was the one relieving myself of the pain, so I had to hear myself speak my words of forgiveness. Now I'm at peace with her memory. She—and I—can finally "rest in peace."

Since I made peace with my mother's memory, my feelings of forgiveness toward my mother have evolved, and I have become a different person. I've finally realized that I am entitled to personal happiness, and that realization has changed my life. I have made positive, healthy life changes that have brought me peace and joy and allowed me to help others. My life is completely different from what it was, and I can credit my personal grief recovery work for that growth.

I have seen many others heal after a wandering phase that included grief work and exercises such as the loss history and letter of release. One woman's outlook changed completely after she read her letter out loud, alone, at her mother's grave. Such simple healing actions—making lists and writing a letter—have such a powerful impact.

Say whatever you need to say in your letter of release, but do include the four key points that enable you to forgive, complete your relationship, say good-bye, and release the pain:

1. Thank the person.

2. Forgive the person.
3. Apologize to the person.
4. Say good-bye.

When you have more than one relationship to complete, write a letter of release for each one. Release those who are living and dead. You do not have to limit your letters of release to just people. You can also write these letters to pets, to former jobs, to any situation you have grieved or are grieving. You will be releasing not only who or what you have lost, you will also be releasing those painful emotions that have kept you wandering in your personal desert for so long.

When Healing Comes

We've all been taught how to acquire things: we've been taught how to get an education, a job, a car, a house. Plenty of courses are available to teach us how to get whatever we want. But what education do we receive about dealing with loss? Where can we go to learn to deal with the conflicting feelings caused by significant emotional loss? Loss is so much more predictable and inevitable than gain, and yet we are woefully unprepared to deal with it.

Whether you grieve the death of a loved one, a not-so-loved one, divorce, breakup, job loss, abuse, emotional trauma, loss of trust, or any other kind of loss, the grief and pain you feel can be healed. But it won't magically go away. You must take the steady steps necessary to say good-bye to what you have lost and go on living.

When you can say good-bye to your loss, move on, and regain joy and passion, then you have healed. When you heal, you will:

- Be able to talk about your important losses without tears or fears.
- No longer need to talk about the past with anger.
- Let go of those images that cause you to doubt yourself and your abilities.
- Project a positive self-image to yourself and to the world.
- Create healthy romantic, family, and professional relationships and friendships.
- Raise your kids with love and confidence.
- Learn how to forgive those who have hurt you in the past.
- Freely embrace those who love you.
- Say good-bye to, and make peace with, loved ones and less-than-loved ones.

At the end of your wandering through the desert of grief, you will have your life back. And your losses will have become your life teachers. You will have journeyed from mourning to morning, and you will finally reach your own Promised Land, just like the Israelites of old.

CHAPTER 8

Faith and Strength

The Story: Lessons from the Book of Job

WHAT DO YOU do when you think you have suffered more than anyone should ever have to, when you begin to think that God is testing you by making your life a living nightmare? It is now time to meet my friend Job. He lost everything—his wife, his kids, his cattle, his home. And he survived!

The Old Testament book of Job begins by introducing the man whose name would become synonymous with the concept of faith in the face of terrible loss: "There was a man in the land of Uz, whose name was Job; and that man was wholehearted and upright, and one that feared God, and shunned evil. And there were born unto him seven sons and three daughters. His possessions also were seven thousand sheep, and three thousand camels, and five hundred yoke of oxen, and five hundred she-asses, and a very great household; so that this man was the greatest of all the children of the East."

Job had everything a man could want at the time. And he was a good man, too. He was so conscious of making sure he did right that he regularly made burnt offerings to God on behalf of his sons on the off chance that they may "have sinned, and blasphemed God in their hearts."

One day, "the sons of God came to present themselves before the Lord, and Satan came also among them." God asked Satan where he had come from, and Satan answered, "From going to and fro in the earth, and from walking up and down in it."

God was proud of Job and wondered if Satan had noticed the fine man. God said to Satan, "Has thou considered My servant Job, that there is none like him in the earth, a whole-hearted and an upright man, one that feareth God, and shunneth evil?"

But Satan was not very impressed. He believed that the only reason Job was such a fine, upstanding citizen, and a God-fearing man was that God had protected him, and "hast blessed the work of his hands, and his possessions are increased in the land." Satan theorized that if God took everything away from Job, that righteous God-fearing man would lose his faith in God and would "blaspheme Thee to Thy face."

So sure was God about Job's faith, however, that he offered to test the man. God said to Satan: "Behold, all that he hath is in thy power; only upon himself put not forth thy hand." As long as Satan did not physically harm Job, God would allow Satan to do whatever he wanted to everything that Job had. The test was on.

By the end of the first chapter of Job, Job had lost his oxen, asses, sheep, camels, servants, and, finally, his ten children. Upon hearing of their deaths—they had all been together in the eldest's home when "there came a great wind from across the wilderness, and smote the four corners of the house, and it fell upon the young people"—Job did not curse God. Instead, he worshipped him: "Naked came I out of my mother's womb, and naked shall I return thither: The Lord hath given, and the Lord hath taken away; blessed be the name of the Lord."

Satan went back to see God. Again, God sang Job's praises, adding, "And he still holdeth fast his integrity, although thou didst move Me against him, to destroy him without cause." Still, Satan was not impressed. He figured it was one thing to lose your possessions and children without losing faith in God, but quite another to physically suffer and still have faith. "But put forth Thy hand now, and touch his bone and his flesh," Satan said, "surely he will blaspheme Thee to Thy face."

God agreed to test Job physically, as long as Satan did not kill Job. "Behold, he is in thy hand," God said, "only spare his life." By the end of Job's second chapter, Satan had covered Job with sore boils "from the sole of his foot even unto his crown."

When Job's wife asked him why he wasn't cursing God, he told her she was speaking "as one of the impious women speaketh," and asked her, "What? Shall we receive good at the hand of God, and shall we not receive evil?" He was willing to take the bad with the good.

AND GOD CREATED HOPE

Three of Job's friends heard of Job's misfortunes and came to see him. "So they sat down with him upon the ground seven days and seven nights, and none spoke a word unto him; for they saw that his grief was very great."

After that week of mourning, Job cursed the day he was born, and wondered why he did not just die at birth, but he still did not curse God or lose his faith. Job's friends told him that they thought his losses and suffering were punishments for some kind of sin he must have committed. And they asked him philosophical questions that he could not answer.

They did a pretty bad job of consoling him. Chapter 16 opens with Job's response to their unending pressure. "I have heard many such things," Job said. "Sorry comforters are ye all. Shall windy words have an end?" In chapter 19 Job asks his friends, "How long will ye vex my soul, and crush me with words? These ten times have ye reproached me; ye are not ashamed that ye deal harshly with me."

Job still clung to his faith. Chapter 27 opens with Job reaffirming that faith: "And the Almighty, who hath dealt bitterly with me; all the while my breath is in me, and the spirit of God is in my nostrils, surely my lips shall not speak unrighteousness, neither shall my tongue utter deceit . . . till I die I will not put away mine integrity from me. My righteousness I hold fast, and will not let it go."

In chapters 38–41 God speaks to Job, reminding him of all of his powers, and chastising Job for thinking that his friends might have been right, that he might have been punished for sinning. And in chapter 42 God speaks to

Job's friends: "My wrath is kindled against thee . . . for ye have not spoken of Me the thing that is right, as My servant Job hath."

God was displeased with Job's friends' behavior and words spoken to Job, but he was pleased with Job's handling of his misfortune and grief and his understanding of God. God commanded Job's friends to take "seven bullocks and seven rams, and go to My servant Job, and offer up for yourselves a burnt-offering; and My servant Job shall pray for you."

Job's friends made the burnt offering, Job prayed for his friends, and God accepted the offering and prayers. As the final chapter of Job ends, verse 10 tell us, "The Lord changed the fortune of Job, when he prayed for his friends; and the Lord gave Job twice as much as he had before."

Job's relatives also came to see him and comforted him "concerning all the evil that the Lord had brought upon him; every man also gave him a piece of money, and every one a ring of gold."

God gave Job fourteen thousand sheep, six thousand camels, one thousand yoke of oxen, and one thousand she-asses. And seven sons and three daughters. "And after this, Job lived a hundred and forty years, and saw his sons, and his sons' sons, even four generations. So Job died, being old and full of days."

So you see, Job thought he was being punished, that God was playing with him. When we lose everything, we, too, begin to think just like Job. Our faith falters, and our hope disappears. But remember, no matter how much pain Job suffered, he never lost his faith. He had faith that somehow, someday, everything would be okay.

Faith is not wishful thinking. It is a sincere belief, a certain knowing. We can draw upon strength to have faith that we will move beyond our grief. And we can draw strength from the fact that we've survived losses before. The operating principle of faith can be applied to one loss or to many, simultaneously. It can be applied to anything. The principle never changes, but its applications are infinite.

When you first suffer a loss, in your pain and grief you may moan, "Why did this have to happen? Why me?" Even those who have faith may head in that direction. After all, having faith does not guarantee that bad things won't happen. But you can have faith that ultimately you will heal and be okay, and that circumstances will improve, without attaching that faith to God or anything religious. There's a difference between having faith in God (or another religious figure) and his ability to help you recover from grief and have a nice life, and simply having faith that you will be okay. God is part of the first equation, but not part of the second.

Those people who think they do not have faith (with or without God in the equation) should look back at the times in their lives when they were in pain or suffered a loss and remember that they did recover and life did get better. This will help them to believe—to have faith—that they'll recover from the loss they're dealing with now.

Faith is all about believing in the future, embracing the future's uncertainty, not fearing it. Emotionally strong people are more inclined to not fear the future and to see the possibility of hope in the future, not pain superstitiously associated with the unknown. When you live without strength, and in fear, you believe that the unknown has a high possibility of being bad. But think of every good thing that has ever happened to you. All of those happened in an unknown future. There was a time before, a time when you had no idea about what the future would bring. And it ended up bringing you good things.

That reminds me of the bumper sticker that says: "Today is the tomorrow you worried about yesterday."

Not "Why " the Righteous Suffer, but "How" the Righteous Suffer

Most people think the story of Job is about asking why the righteous suffer and the evil prosper. But I don't think that is what Job is about. Job doesn't address *why* the righteous suffer, it shows us *how* they suffer, because we all suffer.

Job's friends accuse him of committing a sin, and they think his suffering is a punishment for his sin. Later, God is angry with Job's friends, because they've gotten it all wrong.

The story of Job is not about sin. It is about not losing faith in the face of loss, grief, and suffering. Job ultimately discovers that life can be seen as a test of faith. And he comes to a more realistic faith in God in which he understands that having faith doesn't mean that you won't be tested by life's hardships, pain, and suffering.

Anybody can believe in God, or have faith in the future, when they do not suffer any losses. That is easy. The real test is: how do you believe in God, or have faith in the future, when you do have losses and pain in your life?

From the beginning of this story, it is made very clear that Job hasn't sinned and that the bad that will happen to him during this period of his life is not a punishment, but rather a test. Unfortunately, we're all trained to believe that whenever something bad happens to us it must be a punishment from God because we've done something wrong. Job reminds us that evil is not always a punishment, and that people who do not deserve bad things still have to endure them. Stuff happens. Good stuff and bad stuff. Both happen as a matter of course in our lives, not as rewards or punishments from God.

God's purpose for putting Job through everything was not to punish or reward him, or even to judge him. It was a test, and its purpose was to teach him about what faith really is. Although he did not lose his faith in God or curse him, Job did become self-pitying, impatient, and angry. His friends led him in that direction, because they told him that God had punished him for sinning, and Job began to wonder if they were right. He felt that way until he finally decided he wanted to talk directly to God. When Job and God talked, God blasted Job for thinking that he, Job, had any power in how the universe works, meaning that Job did not have the right to think he was being punished for sins, because Job's actions did not have that kind of power over the universe and God. God told Job that his actions do not have the power to cause God to do anything at all, including punishing him.

That takes care of the question about whether what happened to Job—or that happen to anyone else, for that matter—are automatically punishments from God. Neither Job nor anyone else has the power to cause God to do something.

God may punish, but he chooses why, when, how, and who. When God makes those decisions, he is not necessarily reacting to what people do. When and if God does decide to punish, it is his choice only and not an automatic response to bad behavior, sin, or evil. Which is why sometimes we see evil people not being punished.

Evil Is a Test

I have come to this conclusion: evil is a test of the righteous to see if they will do something about it. Sometimes they will, and sometimes they won't. Sometimes they expect someone else to do something about it, sometimes they figure it is God's job to do something about it.

God put us on this earth, but what would be the point if we were all simply his puppets? There is no point in that. He put us here, and he wants to see what we will do in any given situation. When good things and bad things happen to us, he wants to see how we will react. And when evil (which is at the root of so much loss, grief, and suffering) arises, he wants to see what we will do about it. What kind of people are we? Will we tolerate evil? Will we pass the buck and hope someone else does something about it? Will we just sit back and figure that God will take care of it?

God wants us to be responsible. And in the case of evil, for example, we will show our true colors. Evil is an excellent test for the righteous and those who believe they're righteous. Just how righteous are you? Will you do anything—or nothing—in the face of evil? This is a great way for God to see what each and every one of us is made of.

Every time I hear a dictator say something cruel or dangerous, I think of it as a test. Will anyone have the strength to stand up and challenge it? Will those who say something to challenge it actually do something to challenge it? Will people claim they would like to do something—because what they've seen or heard seems so awful—but then come up with excuses why they can't do anything about it? Look at all the genocides and mass murders and all the countries that either did nothing to try to stop them or waited until thousands or millions of people died before saying or doing anything.

This plays out not just on a global, national, or local scale, but also within families, among friends, and in the workplace. When evil makes itself known, often in the form of cruelty or abuse, what will people do? This is God's test: what will you do in the face of evil?

Faith, Strength, Consolation, and Mourning

When Job's friends first came to him, the only good thing they did was to initially be quiet. They sat in silence with him for a week. But then they began to berate him. So they ended up being terrible comforters, even though they started out the right way.

The best way to comfort someone at the beginning of mourning is to give the person a hug, say you are sorry for his or her loss, ask if there's anything you can do to help, and then shut up. Let them do the talking or let them be silent—the choice is theirs.

Unless a mourner is in deep trouble—acting or talking suicidal; posing a possible harm to others; in danger of abusing drugs, alcohol, or anything else addictive, including shopping, sex, or gambling—or asks for your advice or opinions, do not take charge and tell the person what to do, think, or feel.

Instead of comforting Job, his friends blamed him for his misfortune. After God told Job that his misfortune was not punishment, we know that Job understood God's words, because when God asked him to pray for his friends, he willingly complied. Job realized that God was right, and his friends had been wrong: Job was not being punished. When Job prayed for his friends, he knew that God had asked him to do so because his friends were wrong and needed to be prayed for. It is interesting to note that Job's friends never prayed for him in his time of need, they just blamed him.

After Job prayed for his friends, God began to restore Job's losses. It was only after Job stopped thinking he might be a terrible sinner and started praying for his misguided friends that God gave Job everything he had previously lost.

Even though Job hadn't lost his faith in general, he had lost faith in himself. Once he got that back, God gave him back everything that had been taken from him, and then some.

This is central to the question *How should we mourn?* When we're grieving, we naturally feel like the center of the universe, but that also brings with it some incorrect, negative ideas and emotions: we may think we're responsible for our misfortune, and we can feel guilty. The lesson from Job is that even in the midst of loss and grief, you do not have to see yourself as a victim, as a guilty party, as the biggest loser in the universe. Your healing will only come when you let go of those notions. It's okay to be the walking wounded for a little while, and to take the loss personally—"He died on me!"—but only when you begin to let that go will the true healing begin.

The book of Job teaches us the lesson "How do the righteous suffer?" by showing us that faith helps you when you are grieving—faith that everything will ultimately be okay, and faith in yourself. When you have faith and strength, it doesn't mean you are not going to feel bad. It just means you believe you will recover and have a fulfilling life.

When you say to someone, "Have faith that everything is going to be okay," how do you define *okay*? What's "okay" to one person is awful to another. Does "okay" mean as good as it was before the loss and the grief? Does "okay" mean what was different before the loss and the grief, but still fulfilling? Does "okay" mean worse than things were before the loss and grief, but at least not terribly awful? Just what is "okay," anyway?

When we say "Everything's gonna be okay," or "You are gonna be okay," what we really mean is, "You are not going to die from grief; you will survive this and put together a new life."

What will the quality of that new life be? In large part, that is up to the griever. Remember, loss is not the issue, it is how we deal with it that is the issue.

The Valley Overshadowed by Death

One of the verses in the 23rd Psalm says: "Yea, though I walk through the valley of the shadow of death, I fear no evil for Thou art with me." The actual translation is "the valley overshadowed by death," so when you think about that phrase, this line of the psalm is even more applicable to those who are grieving.

When we say that God is our shepherd, it means God guides us and will take care of us the way a shepherd looks after his flock of sheep. And when we're walking through "the valley overshadowed by death," we do not need to be afraid, because God is with us. When you are grieving, you are walking through that valley.

You may not be comforted by that idea and prefer a different approach, believing that if God was so concerned about your well-being, you wouldn't have suffered this loss, or he would've stopped it or somehow made it less painful. Perhaps you don't even know if you believe in God. If either of these are the case, you can substitute any name for the word *God*. Think of surrounding yourself with the support of those who care about you and can console you. Think about one or more of them, or all of them, as the "shepherd" looking after you.

You can also think in more spiritual terms without defining the shepherd as God. You can think of the shepherd as the universe, as life, looking out for you. You can think, as many people do when they feel a connection to nature and the universe, that you are never alone, because you have an entire universe around you that interacts with you and responds to you. You can gain comfort and strength from nature, in particular, by drawing strength from being surrounded by trees, water, the mountains, the desert, birds, animals, whatever comforts you. (You will recall Bob, from chapter 3, who began to emotionally heal after his harrowing 9/11 experience at the World Trade Center only after he left New York and spent some time alone in the mountains.)

Do, and surround yourself with, whatever brings you comfort, strength, and faith.

Faith and the Future

I have always remembered a kid I knew in summer camp when I was fourteen, who, when he prayed, did not say, "*Baruch Atah Adonai,*" which translates to "Praised are you, O Lord." instead, he said, "*Baruch Atah future.*"

"The future isn't God," I told him.

"Well, I don't know about God," he replied. "But I do know about the future."

He didn't mean that he could predict the future; he meant that he knew the future would come: he had faith that he'd wake up the next morning, that tomorrow would be another day. He knew that the future is an open book and what we make it. That it is an opportunity for life to change, to get better.

He had a positive view of the unknown, of the future. He was excited about what the future could bring. He saw the future as a wrapped gift with a bow. He did not know what was inside, but he knew it could be good, so he was eager to open it. He went to bed every night certain he'd wake up the next morning. He had faith in it, he believed it. He knew the future was there waiting for him. He did not know if God was there or not.

Certainly, you can have faith in God, but you can also have faith in the future, in yourself, and faith in general that you will get through the difficult times and that everything will be okay. Remember, *faith* is just another word for *believe*. It is a knowing, a certainty. Job taught us that. Use the word *believe* in place of the word *faith* and you will see how this works: *I believe I will get through the difficult times, and everything will be okay.*

CHAPTER 9

Forgiveness

The Story: God Forgives Cain, from the Book of Genesis

⌒

BE HONEST NOW. When someone you love died, whether that death was expected or not, weren't you just a little bit angry with that person for dying? How could she do this to me? How will I cope without him? It's okay, anger is a normal first response to grief, and it is the best well-kept secret shared by all mourners. After all, you loved that person and shared a life with him or her all these years, and now you may be all alone. And the worst part of this is: you can't talk with anyone about your anger! If you even hint about these thoughts about being angry with your husband or wife or best friend for dying, you will be considered a horrible person and an embarrassment to your family. They will think, *How selfish of you to think only of yourself at this painful time in our lives!* It is hard to even surface the feeling of anger with a loved one who has died. But trust me, you are not alone. Anger is an ancient and noble sentiment; it goes back all the way to the beginning of the Bible, to the story of the first murder.

After Cain killed his brother, Abel, God forgave Cain, and although he sent him out to wander, he protected him. In letting Cain live, it was as if God had said to him, "We've seen what you can destroy, now let's see what you can create." Cain's descendants became the "fathers" of cities, arts, and sciences. Since they essentially became the "fathers of civilizations," we see that plenty of good came out of God's decision to forgive Cain.

Forgiveness is one of the first lessons in the Bible. When you are grieving, all forms of forgiveness are essential to your healing, including forgiving yourself and those who have died. One of my favorite ideas about forgiveness is the Grief Recovery Institute's definition of forgiveness: "Giving up the hope for a different or better yesterday." When you can do that, you have forgiven someone or yourself.

When people die, we feel cheated. We did not have enough of them, they died too soon (even if they're elderly), and we feel we've been cheated out of all the time we thought we would have to spend with them, out of all the days we thought we would be able to spend with them.

When people die, then, we're angry. And that anger is the deep, dark, dirty secret of grief. We're angry with them for dying, so we need to forgive them for dying, and we need to forgive ourselves for being angry.

Death is very inconvenient. People typically do not die when it's convenient for them or for us. Look at all the older widows who have no idea what to do with finances, bills, and insurance policies. Those women came of age in a generation when husbands took care of such tasks, and it

never occurred to the husbands or wives that one day—
maybe sooner than anyone ever thought—the wives would
have to take care of the finances. Do those men think
they're going to live forever? Why don't they let their
wives know what's going on? When those women were
teenagers, they had better life skills than they have when
they become older widows.

The baby boomer widows will be different, because,
unlike their parents' generation, these women haven't been
kept in the dark about such matters, and most have had
careers and lived on their own as adults before marrying.

The men of the boomers' parents' generation haven't
fared much better in widowhood than the women. When
a wife dies, the husband is clueless about how to dress
himself, feed himself, and take care of the house. He has
no idea what his wife has been doing all these years to take
care of him and their home.

Recently, an eighty-three-year-old man I know lost his
wife. He has no idea how to do the laundry, so he's hired a
woman to do it. He eats out six nights a week, because his
wife did all the cooking, and he is completely lost in the
kitchen. He lives in the Northeast and spends his winters
in Florida. After she died, he had no idea what to do to get
ready to go to Florida. "My wife always packed for me and
got everything done before we left," he told me. "All I had
to do was bring the car around." Death has been very inconvenient for all of these older widows and widowers.

Are some of them angry that they've been left behind,
alone, to fend for themselves? You bet they are. No matter

how old we are or what our circumstances are, we're angry when we've suffered a loss.

Unfortunately, anger is much easier to ignore than it is to deal with. So people stay angry. And even if they want to do something about it, most people don't even know where to begin. To top it all off, they're also angry with themselves—guilt-infused anger—for feeling anger toward their dead loved ones. They would rather not feel this way, but since they don't know how to make it go away, they just bury their feelings beneath the surface and go on.

All that anger comes from focusing on yourself instead of on the person who died. You are grieving, so it's only natural for you to focus on yourself, and this creates a double grief: You're grieving for the one who died as well as for yourself.

How do people get out of this mess? By forgiving both themselves and those who have died. Or if they're grieving a breakup, by forgiving both themselves and those they have lost. But since most people have no idea how to do that—forgiveness is a confusing and tricky business—they substitute (and get stuck in) other behaviors to try to cover their grief-induced and guilt-induced anger, escaping through drugs, food, alcohol, sex, depression, hibernation, over-socializing, anger with other people, and even suicide.

Learning to Forgive

When you draw upon your strength and say, "I'm not going to let this destroy the rest of my life," you can deal with the anger and keep going instead of allowing the loss and resulting anger ruin the rest of your life.

What's the best way to handle your anger with a loved one who's died? And how can you deal with the guilt-infused anger you feel toward yourself for being angry with them? If you haven't already done the exercises in chapter 7 of this book, the loss history and the letter of release, go back and do them now. If you have done both exercises and feel that you are on your way to forgiveness, then the rest of this chapter will serve to reinforce that. If you have done those exercises but still feel you have not forgiven your loved ones and yourself, assess where you are right now:

- Are you on the path to forgiveness?
- Have you begun working on forgiveness and gotten stuck?
- Have you tried and tried, but feel you are still far from forgiving?

If your answer to any one of these questions is, "Yes," then you may want to go back and complete the loss history and letter of release again. Forgiveness is a process and everyone moves through it at his or her own individual pace.

The rest of this chapter will help you understand the forgiveness process. To begin, let's look at God and Cain: God forgave Cain for killing Abel, but Cain did not even realize that God had forgiven him. That is the model for forgiveness: *When people die or leave, you can forgive them, and it still works, even though they do not know they've been forgiven.*

After all, dead people can't know that you've forgiven them. The pain of the relationship is *your* pain—they're dead. And those who have otherwise left you have emotionally moved on. Again, the pain of the relationship is your pain, not theirs. Therefore, in those cases the work of forgiveness is yours.

Forgiveness, like love, must be unconditional in order to be real. Let's look at some familiar scenarios that we associate with what we consider forgiveness:

- If someone asks for your forgiveness, you find it easy or easier to give. If someone doesn't ask for forgiveness, you find it difficult or impossible to give.
- If the person explains so that you understand what's behind what hurt or angered you, you find it easy or easier to forgive. If the person doesn't explain, and you do not understand, you find it difficult or impossible to forgive.
- You find it easy or easier to forgive someone who's never hurt or angered you, or rarely does. You find it difficult or impossible to forgive someone who has hurt you many times before. Or you've developed the habit of "forgiving" an emotionally or physically abusive person, and you equate the word *forgiveness* to the concept of being a victim and putting up with disrespect or abuse.
- If there's "something in it" for you, you find it easy or easier to forgive. If there isn't "something

in it" for you, you find it difficult or impossible to forgive.

None of those scenarios exemplifies authentic forgiveness, because all of them attach conditions to that forgiveness.

- Forgiveness does not equal being a victim or putting up with abuse. You should leave all disrespectful and abusive people and situations.
- When you forgive, that does not mean you condone the actions of the person who hurt or angered you, even when that person is you.
- When you forgive, that does not mean you forget.
- When you forgive, that does not mean it is okay that the person hurt or angered you.
- When you forgive, you are not doing the other person a favor, *you are doing yourself a favor.*

Just what is forgiveness? When you forgive, you let go of your hurt or anger, and you do not carry it around with you anymore. You make peace with what happened. Forgiveness happens inside of you and, believe it or not, has nothing to do with the other person or even the particulars of the situation. This is why other people—whether they are dead or alive—do not even have to know that you've forgiven them. And it is why you can forgive without being asked. When you forgive, you have unconditionally decided not to carry that particular piece of baggage anymore. That is all that forgiveness is.

Forgiveness is defined by the *Merriam-Webster Dictionary* as: "To give up resentment of." Resentment is what's in that baggage you let go of.

Forgiveness is part of completing the relationship with the person who died or is no longer in your life. Of course, you will be completing that relationship in your head. Even if you have had closure conversations with the person you lost before the death, or before, during, or after the breakup, you will still need to finish completing the relationship. You do that alone, in your head, even if you receive assistance by talking with a wise, trusted friend, family member, or professional. The loss history and letter of release (again, see chapter 7) help you complete your relationships with those you have lost, and help you "lay them gently down."

When you've completed the "old" relationship, you are freed from it. You can now begin a "new" relationship with that person. Are you surprised to hear that you have a new relationship with someone who has died or is no longer in your life? Of course, it is nothing like the old one. The person you lost has been recast and now plays a different role in your life. One of the definitions of *relation* is "someone you are connected to." You have a connection to the one you lost, even if that connection is viewed from the perspective of the past—and is defined as a former connection—and you never have anything to do with that person again.

You can have many different kinds and levels of connection with those you have lost, whether they're alive or not, whether you share an active friendship or not, whether you ever communicate with, or see them again or not.

Forgiveness in Action

Cain was out in the world, not knowing that God had forgiven him. He did not ask for God's forgiveness, and God did not tell him that he'd forgiven him. God also forgave himself for giving Cain free will, which is what led Cain to kill Abel. Free will can lead to plenty of good, but it can also lead to evil. This means that free will can lead to either destruction or forgiveness. When you do not forgive, you destroy your life, your world, bit by bit. But when you forgive, your life changes, and you end one way of life and automatically begin another.

God also forgave himself for creating an imperfect world. His perfect world—the Garden of Eden—was gone, and in its wake was born the new, imperfect world in which we live. Back in Eden, Abel had been a shepherd, and Cain had been a farmer. Maybe Cain's job was to go out and create a new garden, a new paradise to take the place of the Eden that no longer existed. This new paradise wouldn't be perfect, but it would be the world he'd be living in after Eden, and he had to go out and help create it. Maybe that act of creating his new environment, his new "garden," was how Cain forgave God. Cain made himself a new life, and that is part of the definition of forgiveness, because he "gave up the hope of a different or better yesterday" and moved on without holding onto old baggage.

Sometimes people think they've forgiven and moved on, but they really haven't, because they're still hoping to change yesterday, still clinging to the old baggage. That is not moving on.

According to Rabbi Harold Kushner, we should forgive people, even those we don't like, so that we don't give them, and that anger we carry, so much power over us. This is good, standard psychological advice. When you're angry with the dead, it isn't hurting the dead, it's only hurting you. And when you're angry with the living, it eats away at you even though they have moved on.

Time is unforgiving unless you do something with it. Forgiveness doesn't just happen by itself because time has passed. You must use that time to do the forgiving. Nothing will get better with time unless you use that time to make it better. Because the hurt and anger come from focusing on yourself, the forgiveness must also come from focusing on yourself.

How does time operate in forgiveness? We take small steps, over time, that lead us to forgive people and to forgive ourselves. You don't just forgive all in one day. Forgiveness is a process.

We often find it more difficult to forgive ourselves than others, because we feel guilty. That just makes forgiveness even harder. With guilt comes regret and "if onlys." *If only I had done things differently, this wouldn't have happened. If only the situation had been different, I wouldn't have done what I did.*

Again, we're dealing with the idea that forgiveness is tied to giving up the hope of a different or better yesterday. In this way, the past becomes a memory, not a prison.

When Forgiveness Seems Impossible

One of the biggest challenges you may ever face is to forgive yourself when you are responsible for, or believe that your actions contributed to, someone's death.

When Cain killed Abel, God felt guilty. Why? Because in Genesis God created humans and at first didn't tell them not to kill. God had never told Cain not to kill anyone, never told him that killing was a sin. Perhaps part of God's process of forgiving himself, as well as Cain, was that when he tossed Cain out of Eden, he protected him as he wandered and made a new life for himself. Cain's descendants then became the "fathers of civilizations."

Forgiving the Mercy Killer Who Can't Forgive Himself

I spoke with a father who had shot his little girl in a "mercy killing." As the result of an accident, her brain had been so damaged that she had no hope of improvement or recovery. She was beyond vegetative. She was on and off a ventilator, suffered numerous medical complications, and her shoulder had been broken when a nurse improperly turned her. That was the last straw for her devoted, grieving young father. He shot her as she lay in her hospital bed, and she died instantly. Then he waited for the police to take him away.

Although he had wide public support—even among law enforcement, the justice system, and his jurors—this devastated father could never forgive himself as others had. He spent a number of years in prison, where even the most cold-blooded among his fellow inmates showed him compassion, and then he was released. He still hadn't forgiven himself.

Although he perceived that he took his daughter's life in order to end her suffering, he could not let go of one thought: what if he had caused her pain when he shot her? When your heart is broken, appealing to your head rarely works, so logic could not console him: because of her severe brain damage, she almost certainly felt nothing, and even if she had felt something, the pain would have lasted just a second—nothing compared to the pain her father wanted to end, the pain she had endured for months.

To numb his pain, he took pills. He married again (he and his first wife divorced after the mercy killing), but his addiction and his grief drove his second wife away. Whenever the pills wore off, he would feel his emotional pain again, his unending grief, his inability to forgive himself. So he made sure he stayed numb on pills all the time. He went into rehab, but resumed his addiction when he was released, because he still had his grief and his pain. He still needed his pills to numb him.

Will his story have a happy ending? Will he ever forgive himself, recover from his grief, and end his pain and his addiction? I don't know. It's been more than twenty years since his little girl died, and he has just completed drug rehab again. And just as important, he has begun to talk about forgiveness in a way he never thought about before—as a possibility. He believes that his daughter has forgiven him, and that God has, too. He's begun to see that he has value, that he can be forgiven by the one person whose forgiveness he needs the most: himself.

One Man's Dark Night of the Soul

A colleague recently told me the touching story of country-and-western singer Dale Watson's journey through grief and forgiveness, which is chronicled in the film documentary *Crazy Again,* and in the memoir *I'd Deal with the Devil to Get Her Back,* which he has just finished writing.

In September 2000, Dale was looking forward to a future with his beloved soul mate, Terri. Late one night, after an argument between the two, a distraught Terri was driving from Austin to Houston, where Dale would be performing the next night. She tried to reach him on his cell phone, but he had left it in his van while he and his band were eating in a restaurant after that night's gig.

Little more than a half hour outside of Austin, Terri lost control of the car, it flipped numerous times, and she died instantly. Receiving word of her death the next morning, Dale was inconsolable. He blamed himself for her accident: *If only we hadn't had that disagreement, she wouldn't have been upset and driving. If only I'd had my cell phone with me.*

Despite the comfort and support of his family, friends, colleagues, and an entire industry, Dale could not get past his grief and could not forgive himself. He and Terri's mother consoled each other, but Dale still could not begin healing.

A few months later, on New Year's Eve, he tried to commit suicide with sleeping pills, but it didn't work. He received therapy after that, and it looked like he was finally beginning the grief healing process. But that was just an illusion. He was going through false grief recovery actions: he thought he had let go, but he hadn't.

During the next eighteen months, Dale immersed himself in religion, spirituality, metaphysics, and New Age philosophies as an attempt to continue his relationship with Terri rather than complete it. He dedicated himself to trying to contact her in the afterlife, but it wasn't out of healthy curiosity or for closure. He did not want to heal and move on. He read books, visited psychics who claimed contact with "the other side," and tried, himself, to make contact. This led him to trying a Ouija board early in the summer of 2002. It was downhill from there.

Believing he'd made contact through the Ouija board with not only Terri but a spirit guide, Jesus, and a host of angels as well, Dale believed everything "they" told him. He decided that as long as no one got hurt, he would do whatever these spirits told him to do so that he could please God and one day go to heaven to be with Terri. But someone did get hurt: Dale. His spiritual journey grew into a dark night of the soul. His communications with the spirits intensified as their method changed from the Ouija board to automatic writing and, finally, to voices in his head.

As he and his band toured the United States and Europe in the summer of 2002, Dale led a double life: performer and a man on a spiritual mission. That mission—given to him by the "spirits"—led him from preparing to announce Judgment Day, to running a council in heaven, to an attempt to deliver to the pope a new manuscript from Jesus—all of this playing out in his head. Every day, he questioned his sanity, wondering, *Am I nuts? Do I have an overactive imagination? Or could this all be real?*

After a battle with the devil, Dale's breakdown became a breakthrough. When he symbolically triumphed over evil, Dale was finally able to begin letting go of guilt and move toward forgiveness and grief recovery. His breakdown had been a form of post-traumatic stress disorder, triggered by his intense unresolved grief and guilt. And it led him to finally recover and to complete his relationship with Terri.

Dale seems to be much better now, and through his music he teaches others the life lessons of forgiveness that he himself has learned. I do wonder, however, if he has ever admitted any anger toward Terri. After all, it does take two to have an argument, and had she not contributed to their disagreement, she might still be alive today. And had she not lost control of her car, they probably would be husband and wife today. Is there anger? Perhaps he has simply bypassed any angry feelings, or perhaps he has hidden them deep down in his soul, or perhaps those feelings will yet appear. Only time will tell, and I wish him well. I just still wonder.

Forgiving the Unforgivable

How can we forgive ourselves, and others, when we believe we're faced with the unforgivable? When asked how anyone could forgive something as horrendous as the Holocaust, Rabbi Shlomo Carlebach famously said, "If I had two hearts, I would dedicate one of them full-time to hating the Germans. But I only have one heart, and I am not going to waste it on such nonsense as hate."

When we choose not to forgive, to let go, we're the ones who suffer, not those we do not forgive. And when we choose not to forgive ourselves, the pain is twice as bad.

What Forgiveness Feels Like

How do you know if you have forgiven someone? Or yourself? You feel lighter, happier, freer, like your life is yours again and doesn't belong to the person you needed to forgive, or to the guilt you carried if that person was you. You feel like you have your life back. You are not actively angry anymore. When the other person's name is mentioned, a dagger doesn't go through your heart or the pit of your stomach anymore. Yesterday is at peace, and it is not contaminating today.

I hope that is how God felt after he forgave Cain and

then himself. Who can ever know? But I do know that when we forgive others and ourselves, we do feel as if we have recovered from a long-term infection with a high fever. We can now breathe easier, we can now lift our head up and smile, because the pain has gone away. We're no longer angry, we are now at peace. And once again life has meaning.

Part Three

FROM MOURNING TO MORNING

CHAPTER 10

Grief without Death

The Story: Passages from the Song of Songs

GRIEF COMES IN many flavors, all of them about loss. Sometimes the loss involves not the death of a loved one, but the breakup of a friendship or the death of a favorite pet. These losses hurt us, too, just as they did King Solomon so long ago. The Song of Songs (also known as the 'Song of Solomon') was written by King Solomon in his youth when he was in love, and its eight short chapters, all in verse, are beautiful poetic writings about love and yearning for those who are alive, but whom we miss. He uses the phrase "my beloved" quite often in these verses. Metaphorically, your "beloved" is anyone or anything you decide it is.

We grieve all of our losses: not only loved ones who die, but also loved ones we lose to a breakup or divorce, as well as friends, pets, jobs, opportunities, setbacks, financial difficulties, geographical moves, illusions, old ways of doing and seeing things, the list goes on. All of these, to one degree or another, are our beloveds.

Let's begin with mourning the loss of a relationship through a breakup or divorce. You will find that many of these principles and feelings also apply to the other kinds of losses in your life. When we miss the "beloved" we have lost through any kind of relationship breakup or divorce, our pain and grief recovery can be just as intense as when we mourn those who have died.

The Song of Songs recognizes yearning, longing, and passion. In the Jewish tradition, the declaration from the Song of Songs 6:3, "I am my beloved's, and my beloved is mine," is spoken during the marriage ceremony, and it is considered a mitzvah—a blessing, or good luck—if the bride and groom read the Song of Songs to each other on their wedding night.

The Song of Songs 2:10–12 speaks of the beloveds' joy at being together:

> *My beloved spoke, and said unto me:*
> *"Rise up, my love, my fair one, and come away.*
> *For lo, the winter is past,*
> *The rain is over and gone;*
> *The flowers appear on the earth;*
> *The time of singing is come"*

Chapter 3:1–4 speaks of the fear of loss:

> *By night on my bed I sought him whom my soul loveth;*
> *I sought him, but found him not.*
> *"I will rise now, and go about the city,*
> *in the streets and in the broad ways,*

I will seek him whom my soul loveth."
I sought him, but I found him not.
The watchmen that go about the city found me:
"Saw ye him whom my soul loveth?"
Scarce had I passed from them,
When I found him whom my soul loveth:
I held him, and would not let him go

Chapter 5:4–6 speaks of yearning and desperately seeking the beloved:

My beloved put in his hand by the hole of the door,
And my heart was moved for him.
I rose up to open to my beloved;
And my hands dropped with myrrh,
And my fingers with flowing myrrh,
Upon the handle of the bar.
I opened to my beloved;
But my beloved had turned away, and was gone.
My soul failed me when he spoke.
I sought him, but I could not find him;
I called him, but he gave me no answer.

Chapter 5:8 continues that yearning:

I adjure you, O daughters of Jerusalem,
if ye find my beloved,
What will ye tell him?
That I am love-sick.

One of the most famous sections, chapter 8:6–7, sums up love's power:

> Set me as a seal upon thy heart,
> As a seal upon Thine arm;
> For love is strong as death,
> Jealousy is cruel as the grave;
> The flashes thereof are flashes of fire,
> A very flame of the Lord.
> Many waters cannot quench love,
> Neither can the floods drown it

While some relationships end, in part, because neither of the people involved are in love, quite often when a relationship ends, one or both of the people involved are still very much in love. When the relationship is over, but your love continues, you are not just mourning the end of the relationship, you are also nursing a broken heart. And a broken heart is no small matter. In many ways your grief process is no different than if your beloved had died. That is because this is a kind of death: the death of a relationship with someone you love. And that is a profound loss. It may even take you as long to heal from this grief as it would take to heal from mourning a death.

I don't know if we ever "get over" those we love. We just eventually make peace with having lost them. And this is true whether they're alive or not. Do you "get over" your feelings of loss? Eventually, yes. Do you "get over" the *person* you've lost? Of course not. And that is because we do not stop caring about people just because they're gone.

During your grief recovery process, you will deal with the same issues (those explored in the other chapters of this book) you must confront when someone dies. And you will deal with one more: rejection and its blow to your self-worth and confidence.

Your beloved's dying is not a rejection of you. But your beloved's breaking up with you or divorcing you is. And that is because you *feel* rejected, whether your beloved intended for you to feel that way or not. Rejection often leads people to question nearly everything about themselves: their appearance, their personality, their intelligence, their emotional and psychological fitness to be in a relationship, their financial status—you name it.

If you did not want the relationship to end, you may carry a torch for your beloved and hope that one day the two of you will be reunited. That aspect of the mourning can make the whole process more difficult than mourning a loved one who died. We know that the dead aren't coming back. We can't be quite sure about the living.

So part of you thinks that you do not have to "get over" him, because he is coming back, or might come back one day. When you're mourning someone who's alive, you lack the incentive to move on, to recover from your grief. You think you won't have to accept that it's completely over, so you don't. You have unfinished emotional business. And you can carry that torch for a very long time. Some people carry it for the rest of their lives.

Why do people hang on to relationships once they're over? Is it the height of optimism? Is it faith and hope? No, not really, though it may feel that way. The reason is actually a lot more reality-based than that. It's precedent. We've seen people come back before. We've seen it happen with other couples. We've certainly seen it in plenty of movies and TV shows. And we've even had it happen to us before: somebody came back to us, or we went back. So we hope that will happen to us this time, too.

At the beginning, you mourn the fact that you are in this position right now, but you're not yet mourning the death of the relationship, because you hope you won't have to. You hope you will be getting back together with your beloved. If your beloved comes back and you resolve your difficulties, perhaps the relationship can continue. Hopefully, you will not continue with a relationship unless it is an emotionally healthy one. If your beloved doesn't come back, that is when your real grieving begins. That might be a few weeks, months, or even years after the breakup, and you will have an even stronger grief reaction than you did immediately after the breakup, because accepting that it's over—no matter how long that takes—is far more painful. It's also the beginning of the healing process.

Grieving Relationships without Traditional Mourning Support and Rituals

Not only do we not have the kind of support and rituals to help us with a breakup (divorce or relationship) that we have when someone dies, but we also keep clinging to the hope that we will be reunited with our beloveds. When someone dies, a week later nobody would say to the grieving widow, "It's time for you to get out there and date again. You fell off the horse—time to get right back on!" But when you are mourning a breakup, it's not uncommon for people to encourage you to begin dating again almost immediately. Is this the height of ignorance and insensitivity? You bet it is. If someone suggests this to you, immediately, but diplomatically, end the conversation. This is not someone you should confide in or rely on for emotional support. Don't emotionally stress and drain yourself by trying to explain how you feel to people who don't understand.

Why would people say something so insensitive in the first place? The answer is simple, though you may have trouble believing it because you have loved deeply: the people who believe—and say—these kinds of things have likely never been in love. They may think they've been in love, but they haven't. At least not on any level deeper than "Oh, I loved that movie," or "I love those shoes," or "I love that car." It's easy for those people to begin dating again right away, because they're not in mourning. They were never really in love. Only someone who has truly loved can understand that people are not disposable, that when you love someone, you don't just stop loving them after a breakup.

Society gives a lot respect to those who have lost a loved one to death, but not much to those who have lost someone in a breakup. In fact, they're usually treated in a rather cavalier way: "There are other fish in the sea," "You just need to get right back out there and date," "You're not getting any younger." People don't want to legitimize your mourning, because your beloved is still alive. They believe mourning is something we do only for those who have died. They believe your pain is not legitimate, because it is not connected to death. They are wrong. On all counts.

You have suffered as great a loss as someone whose beloved has died: in both cases it's a loss, the relationship with the beloved is over. And that is extremely painful when you're in love. Either way, it's still the death of a relationship.

Some people believe—and would like you to believe—that relationships are just a game. That when you've lost a relationship, you should "get right back into the game." If you don't have deep feelings for the one you lost, you might be able to go out looking for a new man or new woman, or begin dating, right away. But if you try dating immediately after losing someone you love, you'll never properly heal from your loss. You risk significant emotional damage that will prevent you from having a trusting, loving, healthy relationship in the future.

After a breakup, people often think they're helping or consoling you by playing a blame game: "It's your fault he broke up with you, but if you'd just change, you might not get left next time," or "That no-good S.O.B. broke up with you?" People think they're helping by using blame as a tool to encourage you or boost your ego, something they would never do if you were mourning someone's death.

Enter blame territory very carefully. It's healthy to look truthfully at the strengths and weaknesses and good and bad behaviors of you and your beloved, but do not let blame overshadow the validity of your mourning. It is okay to mourn the loss of someone who may not have been good for you, or who may have hurt you. It's just not okay to want to be with that person again. When you love unconditionally, that means you might love someone who is unhealthy for you to be with. There's nothing wrong with loving that person, just do it from afar. There's everything wrong with actually having a relationship with that person. You can't help who you fall in love with. You *can* keep yourself from having a relationship with the wrong person.

It is important to acknowledge how you feel and to mourn everyone you lose—no matter what the circumstances of the relationship—because if you do not mourn them, you will never recover from your grief and get past the loss of the relationship.

Ten Steps That Begin Your Healing

1. Accept that you have lost your beloved. You don't have to like it, you just have to accept it. Denial will only hurt you.
2. Accept that this is not a temporary loss, it's a permanent one. How do you do that when you know that sometimes people do reunite?

You accept that it's over, and you don't have a crystal ball. You don't know the future, you only know about today. And today, it's over. You're in the same position as those people who don't want to accept that their loved ones have died, and by feeling that way they become the walking dead and keep their loved ones more alive than they really are. You must also accept a death. In your case, it's the death of the relationship. You may ask, "Shouldn't I have hope that he or she will come back?" No, you shouldn't. Instead, you should have hope that you will accept your loss, heal, and recover. If at some point in the future your beloved wants to come back, you (having grown from your loss) may not even want to reunite.

Deal with the issue of reuniting only if and when it happens, but for now accept that the relationship is over. That is the only thing you have to work with now—not the possibilities you imagine in your crystal ball. Deal only with the reality of today, not the possibilities of tomorrow.

3. Be honest about the relationship. Why did it die? What did you contribute to its death? What did your beloved contribute to its death? Were you in love with the wrong person? We can love people with whom we

aren't compatible, or the two of you may just be good people who don't fit together.

While you mourn your beloved, you may find that you're not mourning the circumstances of the relationship, especially if the relationship was abusive, difficult, or unfulfilling. It's not uncommon to love someone and mourn the loss, but to be relieved that the relationship is over. You miss your beloved, but you don't miss the bad relationship. Relationship mourners often would like to have the beloved back, but with the circumstances of the relationship changed. Who wouldn't want to have the magic wand that would bring their beloved back and make the relationship wonderful this time? But for that to happen, the beloved would have to turn into someone completely different—someone capable of making a good relationship with you.

We miss two things and mourn two things simultaneously: the person and the relationship. Separate them in your mind and take an honest look at them. Some people don't mourn the loss of their beloved, they mourn the loss of a relationship, even if that one didn't work. They miss being in a relationship, and having someone else around.

4. Stop seeing the world through the eyes of a broken-hearted person who just ended a

relationship or got dumped. Instead, see the world through the eyes of a person with a future. You may feel like a walking wound, but you're not. You're a person with a wound. Identify with more than just your wound. Don't label or judge yourself. Don't see yourself as a rejected person. Don't see yourself as "all alone" just because you're not part of a couple right now. And never see yourself as damaged goods or unlovable.

5. You don't have a sign hanging around your neck that says, "I've been dumped," or "Loser," so don't carry yourself in the world as if you do.

6. Be honest and look at the lessons you've learned, or need to learn, from this relationship so that they can help you with future relationships.

7. Be clear about who you miss: do you miss your beloved as he is? Or do you miss the person he was, or you thought he was, or hoped he'd be? Separate your beloved's reality from your wishful thinking or illusions. Don't make excuses for bad behavior or have such low expectations that you believe that an abusive, neglectful, selfish, or uncaring beloved was just fine and the only problem was that your expectations were too high. Remember, your less-than-loving beloved trained you to think that way.

8. Even if you had a very nice beloved, remember that if your relationship was healthy and terrific, it wouldn't have ended. Good relationships do not end. Breakups are a blessing in disguise. You may not see it now, but you will in the future. You've "dodged a bullet," as the saying goes. It's hard to feel this at the beginning of your mourning, because pain blinds you to many aspects of reality, including this one.

9. Don't torture yourself with "if onlys."

10. Surround yourself only with supportive people who understand you and can comfort you now, not people who judge you or take your pain lightly. Don't open up to people who aren't supportive.

Grieving Our "Living" Losses

We have more other kinds of losses—"living losses"—than we do literal deaths. People close to us do not die every week, but we do regularly suffer some kind of loss, even if it is just the loss, or death, of an illusion, a belief, an opportunity, or a personal or professional situation. So we spend more of our time mourning—to some degree or another—these losses than losses due to the death of a loved one.

Some of these losses are bittersweet. We're always losing an old way of seeing things and discovering a new way of looking at them. That is called growth. It is healthy to grow and go through changes, even if it can sometimes feel uncomfortable at first. Afterward, we're always happy we gained that wisdom.

When we move from one city to another, we look forward to the new experiences but will miss our old friends and home. Even when we choose to leave a job, we will still miss some of its aspects, including some of our colleagues, while we look forward to the new career opportunity.

Healing from the Old Job, Moving to the New

When we're fired or laid off, we often feel the same way we do when we've been through a relationship breakup or divorce we didn't want. Very few people haven't lost a job. It's a familiar story. I've been through it before, and so, very possibly, have you.

A few years ago, the personnel committee of the synagogue where I'd been the rabbi for six years told me they were recommending that the synagogue not renew my contract. I could have contested their decision by going public to the entire congregation, but I decided that if my leadership did not want me to be their rabbi anymore, then I would leave. And then came the grief.

Why didn't they want me anymore? What had I done, or not done, that displeased them? How had I failed them? Did this mean that I was a "bad" rabbi? A "bad" person? And even worse—did they finally "find me out" and recognize me as the imposter I'm sometimes afraid I am? Every professional, at one time or another, falls prey to "The Imposter Syndrome," feeling that perhaps we're not "the real thing."

I had little idea how I might have failed my congregation, and myself, and I felt that a little piece of me had died. Although I knew that rabbis move from congregation to congregation quite often, whether they want to or not, and that a rabbi staying at one congregation for his entire career has gone the way of an employee staying at one company for his entire career, I was still disappointed and grieving.

I would be job hunting again. Who needed that kind of hassle? While still at the old synagogue, I went through interviews with synagogues around the country as they sized me up, trying to determine if I'd be a good fit for their congregation, while I tried to figure out if they would be a good fit for me.

I had lost something: a piece of myself, my dignity, my honor, my feeling of job satisfaction. How would I mourn? Would I be angry and not talk to people I'd known for six years? Would I trash my congregation's leadership and hope they would be cursed by getting a new rabbi who was incompetent and ineffectual, all flash and no substance? Would I begin to gossip about those who fired me? Well, that is how I felt, and it was perfectly normal for me to feel that way. I was hurt and in pain, and I was looking for a focus for my anger.

But I also knew that if I left angry I wouldn't be completing my relationships with my congregants and friends, and I would continue to carry my grief over those relationships, as well as my anger, with me when I began my new rabbinic position. Before I began my new job, I had to be completely cleansed of, and healed from, the old one.

I had to consciously set out to leave in a good way, and I did. What was the secret of my "good leaving"? I spoke about it publicly, positively, and continually, right up until the day I left. You see, not only was I saying good-bye, but I had to help my friends and supportive congregants say good-bye, too. Talking about leaving allowed all of us to mourn, celebrate, and heal. At first, it was incredibly difficult for me to do this, but it did get easier as the months went on. Not everything went smoothly, however, especially when I went on interviews at other synagogues and was turned down in favor of younger and more handsome candidates. Who knew that a baby boomer rabbi is now considered old, and who knew that rabbis are now supposed to look more like Brad Pitt than like Moses? But ultimately everything turned out well.

The end of the story is that I got a new job. My new congregation fell in love with me, and I fell in love with them. My gifts fit their needs, and vice versa. I emotionally concluded my relationship with my former congregation and was ready to begin again. Had I not left healed, I would have been paralyzed in the future.

Friends Aren't Always Forever

We often think that every friend who comes into our lives is supposed to stay there until one of us dies. While we can, and do, have friends for life, not every friend is forever. The end of a friendship has much in common with the end of a romantic relationship: the same sense of loss, hurt, frustration, regret, anger, betrayal, and disappointment.

My friend Nancy reflects back on two friendships that have ended, each in a different way, with each having taught her different lessons about loss, healing, and what makes a healthy relationship. All of her life, Nancy valued her friendships with both women and men, and made them priorities. She's still close to college and high school friends and friends she made more than forty years ago when she was in elementary school. Although she had mourned the passing of many friends who had died, she had never had a "living loss" of a close friend until she was in her early forties.

Nancy and Ann met when both were in their late twenties and working in similar fields. They first bonded over "shop talk," and their common professional interests, but soon found they had a lot in common personally, too. They socialized together, became friends with each other's friends, confided in each other, and were even bridesmaids in each other's weddings. For more than ten years, hardly a day went by that they didn't have a long conversation.

Shortly after Ann got married, she and her husband moved across the country, where he'd landed his dream job. For about two years, Ann stayed in touch regularly and visited her "old" city, where she and her husband not only had "old" friends, but plenty of family, too. After Ann and her husband had a baby, though, everything abruptly changed.

"Ann announced to me very matter-of-factly over the phone one day that she had 'moved on,'" Nancy recalls. "She said that she had a new life now and was not keeping in touch with any of her friends from before she moved. The way she said that sounded so cold, as if she'd fired a bunch of employees whose services were simply no longer needed. I had a feeling that if I was the only one left that she was keeping in touch with, my time as her friend was probably running out, too."

And it was. Ann's calls became less frequent, the conversations less personal. When Nancy called, Ann would wait weeks before calling back. The birthday cards and Christmas cards stopped coming. "We never did have a conversation in which she gave me the old heave-ho," Nancy says, "But we didn't have to. I got the message loud and clear when she stopped calling and didn't return my phone calls. What hurt the most was that she and I had never even had a disagreement, much less an argument or a falling out. She simply killed a perfectly good friendship."

Nancy tried to rekindle the relationship for a while, but after about a year she gave up. "I guess I was mourning the death of the friendship during that year that I continued to reach out. I'd go for months without calling, then I'd call and leave a light-hearted message on her voice mail. But she didn't call back. Maybe six months later I left another message. And she didn't call back. After a year, I just stopped. That was four years ago."

Nancy felt the classic combination of emotions: hurt and anger. "I'm probably still angry," Nancy admits.

> Maybe it's because I'm one of those people who likes closure. I want to know why she ended our friendship.

I guess I want it to make sense. But I do realize that even if I got that closure, even if we had a conversation abut her ending the friendship, it's not like it would make sense to me. It's a catch-22. Maybe I just want to hear her say it out loud, even though that wouldn't change anything and, in fact, would just reinforce to me that underneath everything she's pretty cold and heartless, something I never would've guessed when we were friends. She was always warm, caring, funny, and never difficult.

The betrayal and rejection we feel when friendships end like this—and so many of them do—can make us question everything about the validity of the friendship. But, no, we weren't nuts. We had that friendship, and it was real, and it was everything we thought it was . . . until one day when it abruptly ended. As Nancy says:

People define friendship differently. Apparently, Ann's definition of friendship was so much different than mine. For her it was a matter of convenience, and that is all. What helps me not take it personally is that she didn't just end our friendship, she ended all of the close friendships she had with those from her "old" life. And it's not that there was anything wrong with that life. I could understand if it had been dysfunctional, painful, or disappointing and she wanted to distance herself from it and everyone associated with it. But, that wasn't the case. She had a great career, wonderful friends, a close family. Some people, though, when they marry, move, or become parents, decide to reinvent themselves and sever all ties. I guess she turned out to be one of those people. That taught me that some people consider friendship to be temporary, simply something to suit their needs for a particular period of time.

When she lost Ann's friendship, Nancy confided in another friend, one who had met Ann, but only a few times. "She wasn't particularly sympathetic," Nancy recalls. "She'd had this happen to her a few times, and was shocked that this was the first time it had happened to me. She said that these days some people bring a cutthroat corporate mentality into their personal lives, and she thought that was what Ann had done. In business everyone is disposable. Even though Ann didn't work in the corporate world, she's a professional, and her so-called friends became as disposable to her as her old business contacts that she no longer needed in her new job in her new city."

In the aftermath of recovering from the loss of her friendship with Ann, Nancy says that she no longer thinks every close friendship has the potential to last a lifetime. "We live in a very disposable culture," Nancy points out. "Everything in society, including our friendships, isn't what it used to be in previous decades. That is sad, but it's the reality. And even though I feel that I'm over this loss, the one thing I'm left wondering about is whether my friendship with Ann was what I'd thought it was. Is anything really ever what we think it is?"

After Ann, the second friend Nancy lost was Marie. That loss felt like a death. Nancy and Marie had been best friends since high school, had gone to college together, and had always been like sisters. But in her thirties, Marie, a married professional, and the mother of two, slipped into substance abuse and has never come out of it. She is in denial, won't admit she has a problem, and won't accept any help. Her husband is a classic "enabler" and won't comfort her, because he knows how angry she'll be with him. So he covers for her.

"The Marie I knew died fifteen years ago," Nancy says.

> I don't know the woman who calls herself Marie, now. Ever since her problem started, she lashes out at anyone who brings it up. She becomes very verbally abusive to the family and friends who've tried to help her. She's shut us all out. I haven't seen her in nearly ten years. Once in a while she calls, but it's difficult to have a conversation with her. When she's high, she makes no sense. When she's sober, she's mean and short-tempered. It's incredibly sad. I literally mourned her as if she'd died. Well, the Marie I knew and loved died a long time ago. She was bright, talented, funny. Now she's someone else entirely, someone I don't recognize. I know she's in pain, but she won't get help and she won't let anyone help her. I'm surprised she's still alive, that what she's been doing hasn't killed her. I know that one day my phone will ring and someone will tell me that Marie is dead. I think what I'll feel most then is relief. That Marie will finally be at peace.

When You've Lost a Pet

While the Song of Songs recognizes the power of our human beloveds, its sentiments can be applied to the devotion we have to the beloved animals we call our friends and family. Mourning the loss of a pet can be a grief without death if your pet has run away or vanished. But if your beloved pet has died, this can be as similar a mourning process as when you are grieving a human loved one.

A woman once said to me, "My dog just died, when can we have the funeral?" I told her that we only do funerals for people. "But I loved him," she said. And it occurred to me that this dog was her beloved. In fact, she had a much better relationship with her loving dog than she had with her hateful husband.

Pets are loved, they're part of the family, and many people are closer to their pets than to most of the humans in their lives, because pets give unconditional love and most people do not. When you are mourning the loss of a pet, most people will give you as much support as they would if you were mourning a human loved one.

I have since changed my mind about how to mark the passing of a beloved pet. Today, if I were asked, I would officiate at that pet's funeral. I'd go to the pet cemetery or conduct a service in which a pet's ashes were to be scattered or kept in an urn. And I'd feel honored to do it.

Honor Your Losses

The losses of all our "beloveds" must be honored and properly mourned, or we can't move on to a healthy, productive, loving future. Our grief recovery process goes on all the time. It is called growth.

CHAPTER 11

Joy

The Story: Lessons from the Book of Proverbs

THESE NEXT TWO chapters are shorter than the preceding ones, and there is a reason. This book is dedicated to the premise—and the promise—that you *can* recover and heal from your losses, that you *can* move on to enjoy life with joy, growth, and wisdom. This book teaches you how to do the work of healing, which is sometimes difficult and always complex. How long will it take to heal? Who knows? That depends on lots of variables, as each one of us is unique. There will be a natural "flow" to your recovery: at first it will hurt plenty, and it may take you awhile to understand what is happening to you. Then you will begin to feel better bit by bit, and life will seem easier. Finally, healing will come, and you will be surprised at its speed.

Like this book, the beginning chapters in your own "healing book" will take you some time, and then, as you begin to feel better, hardly any time at all. When healing comes, as I hope it will very soon, life will become much more manageable, and you will be able to write your own chapters of joy and growth and wisdom, because by then you will "get it," and you will know for sure that you have healed.

Can you laugh when you're in mourning? Is doing so thoughtless and inconsiderate? Do you have to be sad all the time until—*presto*—one day you're healed? Not at all! In fact, as you will soon read, laughter is another doorway to healing, so laugh as much as you can. Proverbs 14:13 says, "The heart may ache even in laughter, and joy may end in grief." You can genuinely laugh and feel joy even when you're grieving. It's healthy to still be able to laugh and be happy about something. At the same time, you should be careful not to live in denial about your grief by hiding behind laughter.

When joy comes knocking, don't close the door in its face out of guilt. Remember that at memorial services and funerals, people don't just cry, they also tell funny stories and laugh. It feels good to have that balance. After all, you don't associate your loved one with only tears and sadness, do you? Let the laughter come—whether it's connected to memories of the one who died, or anything else—and don't feel guilty about moments of joy during grief. They're a blessing.

Just because you've buried someone's body doesn't mean you've also buried their place in your memories. After the funeral or memorial service, when people gather at your home or someone else's, tell those funny stories about your loved one. And continue to tell them for the rest of your life. Wouldn't you want your loved ones to have happiness in their lives after you're gone? Wouldn't you want them to share good memories of you after you're gone? Of course you would.

No matter how far along you are in the grief process, you can only heal when you allow yourself to behave and react as you ordinarily would. So when something amuses you, smile, giggle, and howl with laughter if you want. And surround yourself with the people, activities, and situations that bring you joy. Joy and laughter comfort you when you are grieving.

As George Bernard Shaw said, "Life doesn't cease to be funny when people die anymore than it ceases to be serious when people laugh."

We Laughed and We Cried as Sy Died

Sy Katz died several months ago; he was ninety years old and in rapidly declining health for months. He had been extremely active in my synagogue, serving as the president for many years and continuing to attend services until a month before his death. As the end approached and his illness began to get the better of him, his body began to shut down. His family took him from the hospital to a local hospice, where he lived out his last few days in quiet dignity, surrounded by his loving family—children, grandchildren, and even great-grandchildren! By the way, I highly recommend hospice to all my congregants when their doctors decide that the illness can no longer be treated and that the time has come to allow them to live out their last weeks, months, and sometimes even years free from pain. Sy was unaware of his surroundings, but we were all there with him, telling marvelous stories about him and recounting his exploits, to the delight of all. Did he hear us? Who knows? But supposedly it is our sense of hearing that lasts the longest, so perhaps he did. And even if he didn't hear us, we had a dandy time telling "Sy stories."

Finally the time had come. Sy's breathing was getting increasingly shallow, and it was clear that the end was quickly approaching. As he drew his last breath, we all began to cry as the reality of our loss set in. I asked the family to stand around the bed and hold hands while I prayed the Viddui, Judaism's final confession. I asked God to bless Sy's family, and I thanked God for having shared him with us for so many wonderful years. Then, in an effort to be consoling, I put my arms around Sy's loving wife, Lea, and I prayed something like this: "Dear God, Sy is now free from pain, and he will soon be together in heaven with his beloved parents." Lea lifted up her head, looked at me with tears in her eyes and said, "No, Rabbi, I don't think so! They didn't get along so well!" Well, with that, the laughter exploded in the room, and we were all delirious. The tension had been broken. No one was upset with me, and everyone understood the laughter for what it really was— a welcome break in the sadness and the difficulty of saying good-bye to Sy. The hospice staff was outside wondering just what was going on in that room, and why these crazy people were laughing so hard when their father and husband had just died!

The funeral was held two days later in the synagogue. At one point during the service, all of the women in the family came up together to sing a song that Sy himself had written, a song that extolled the value of his daughters and nieces, titled "*I Am the Goodest of the Girls.*" They sang with tears in their eyes and joy in their hearts, and as you may imagine, it was quite an experience for all of us who were there that day. Sy's life gave us the strength to celebrate even as we mourned. We laughed, and we cried, and it was just fine.

Joy and Guilt

Where does the guilt come from when you have happy moments or laugh while you're mourning? People feel guilty for a number of reasons. Perhaps they feel they didn't do enough for their loved ones before they died, or they have unresolved issues with their dead loved ones. Also, we don't mourn just our loved ones, we also mourn less-than-loved-ones. We may feel guilt associated with aspects of our relationships with those we loved, as well as with those we didn't like very much. You may not have felt any guilt about the relationship when that person was alive, but now that he's dead, you may feel guilty.

Every death means you have no chance to change the relationship. It's frozen as it was when he died. You can't say anything to him and he can't say anything to you. You can't clear up anything, vent, get an apology, give an apology, get an explanation, or give one. It's game over. That never feels good. His death means that emotionally you have to deal with the difficulty of the bad relationship you had with him when he was alive. Your mind fills up with a replay of the whole relationship, something you could keep at bay whenever you wanted when he was still alive. But now that he's dead, there's no tomorrow in which the two of you could improve the relationship. You may feel guilty that you didn't do more to improve it when he was alive, or that as hard as you may have tried, the relationship remained difficult.

You can have a conversation with him in your heart and mind now, and for some people that may work, but for others it's not enough. One of these conversations in your mind just might jump-start the closure and healing process, or give it a good kick when it gets stuck. At any point in your grieving process, such a conversation— even a monologue, since you don't necessarily have to imagine that person responding to what you want to say—can help you finish your unfinished business. I know a woman who flew to Boston, went to her mother's grave, and had a "conversation" with her, and finally, after many years, felt that she had gotten the closure she wanted.

Joy comes with healing steps and with closure. You feel as if a weight has been lifted off you. You literally feel lighter. And you let more joy, happiness, and laughter into your life when you've gotten to the end of the heavy-duty grief, when you feel you've gotten your closure.

Joy without Guilt

Laughter and Healing

You may remember the 1998 Robin Williams movie *Patch Adams,* which focused on the groundbreaking healing-through-humor work of the physician who created the Gesundheit Institute and went on to author *Gesundheit!, House Calls,* and *Illness and the Art of Creative Self-Expression.*

Another pioneer in this field, Norman Cousins, was a magazine editor and the author of a number of acclaimed books covering sociological, political, and cultural issues when he discovered the healing power of humor and laughter. He credited spending a great deal of time watching old classic comedy films with significantly aiding his recovery from what had been a life-threatening illness. He went on to write three books on the impact of humor, laughter, and a positive attitude on healing—*Anatomy of an Illness as Perceived by the Patient* (New York: Norton, 1979), *Healing Heart: Antidotes to Panic and Helplessness* (New York: Norton, 1983), and *Head First: The Biology of Hope* (New York: Dutton, 1989)—and to teach in the field as an adjunct professor of medical humanities for the School of Medicine at the University of California.

Research has shown that laughter is healing. Laughter boosts your immune system, lowers your blood pressure and stress hormones, triggers pain relief, and triggers the release of endorphins, your body's "feel good chemicals." Laughter therapy, also called humor therapy, is now a recognized form of physical as well as emotional healing. Humor and laughter also help you cope, and that is a great benefit when you've suffered a loss, you are grieving, and going through what can be a lengthy recovery process. As Proverbs 17:22 reminds us, "A merry heart is a good medicine, but a broken spirit dries up the bones."

CHAPTER 12

Growth and Wisdom

The Story: Lessons from Psalm 66:10

THE BOOK OF Psalms is a collection of ancient wisdom poems—150 ways of dealing with life's diverse emotions. There are psalms we can recite to encourage us in times of fear, doubt, tragedy, triumph, joy, and hope. Psalm 66:10 shows the growth and wisdom that can come from grief and mourning: "For Thou, Oh, God, hast tried us; Thou hast refined us, as silver is refined." The lesson to all mourners from this verse is: *Because of this loss, I've grown, and I'm a better person. God got me through the difficult times and the grief, and I've been "refined" by the experience.*

When your loved one died, or your relationship fell apart, you probably felt that your life was finished, that you would never recover, that darkness would shadow you forever, that hope was unattainable. Now you know differently, don't you? Some people, after they have gone through a painful loss experience and have learned priceless life lessons about themselves, might even begin to think, "This loss is the best thing that has ever happened to me." Not that they wouldn't for a moment want to be reunited with their loved ones, but now they understand that life goes forward on its own schedule. Loss is part of that schedule, and our task is to adjust to the reality of life and loss.

Loss and grief are growth processes. Since we only learn through loss, and how we respond to loss, then we also only grow through loss, because learning and growing are the same thing. We never stop growing—it is ongoing. Just when you think you've stopped, there's more.

When we grow, we lose the way we used to think and do things, and we discover better, healthier, and more mature ways. Growth is letting go of the old and embracing the new. Since fear—fear of the unknown, the future—is what binds us to the old long after we should have let go, growth is also letting go of fear. We also grow when we wander, when we act on faith, when we forgive, when we let the joy in. Growth, and the resulting wisdom, is the healthy outcome of these challenging aspects of the grief recovery process, no matter what the loss.

Although my father's death, when I was only twelve, was the worst thing that ever happened to me, it was also the best thing that ever happened to me, because of what I learned from it. Would I have learned all of that in some other way? Maybe, but maybe not, since the lessons were so powerful only because the loss of a father is so powerful. What lessons did I learn? Everything I'm sharing with you in this book.

My learning did not take place overnight. My grief recovery and growth process, in fact, didn't even begin until thirty years after my father died, when I was forty-two. That was seventeen years ago. It took so long for me to even begin to heal, grow, and learn because of fear. I was afraid to talk about my father's death and how that loss made me feel. Since most people are uncomfortable talking honestly to us about death and the feelings we have about loss, I didn't have anyone to talk to about how I felt, as far as I could tell, even if I had been inclined to open up. Everywhere I looked with my limited view, I just saw closed doors. As a rabbi, I'd been counseling other people about their losses and grief, but I hadn't dealt with my own.

What finally jump-started my healing and growth was four days that I spent in the company of a grief educator and author as she went from school to school talking to teachers, parents, and kids about death. They spent most of the time telling personal stories of death and loss, talking about how they were affected by their losses, and agreeing that no one had wanted to listen to these stories before now. I was amazed that simply being able to talk about their own losses gave them all a sense of empowerment and peace. The tension melted away as they shared their own grief stories, often through tears and sometimes with laughter. I remember thinking: *is that all there is to be able to heal from loss? Can simply talking about loss be a factor in recovering from that loss?* It seemed so, after I spent those remarkable four days. I knew then that I was on to something important—not only to my congregants, but to me as well.

I always felt that I was good at helping other people deal with their losses, especially the deaths of loved ones, because I understood those firsthand, and now I finally gave myself "permission" to begin to deal with my losses and grief. I knew that the time had come for me to finally deal with my losses. It was the only way I could be the kind of help to others that I wanted to be, to be able to go beyond what I was then offering them.

Not only did I finally begin to deal with my father's death, but I also went on to get yet another academic degree, a Doctor of Ministry, and chose death as the subject of my doctoral dissertation. Then I studied at the Grief Recovery Institute and became a certified grief recovery specialist. By preparing to better help others, I was also furthering my own healing, growth, and learning process.

To Be Whole, First You Have to Break

I'd like to share a story with you that beautifully illustrates how our pain and losses lead us to grow and become better people. Author Steve Goodier tells this story in his book *Joy Along the Way: 60-Second Readings That Make the Trip Worthwhile* (Life Support System Publishing, 2000):

> The story is told of an Eastern village which, through the centuries, was known for its exquisite pottery. Especially striking were its urns; high as tables, wide as chairs, they were admired around the globe for their strong form and delicate beauty.

Legend has it that when each urn was apparently finished, there was one final step. The artist broke it—and then put it back together with gold filigree.

An ordinary urn was then transformed into a priceless work of art. What seemed finished wasn't, until it was broken. So it is with people! Broken by hardships, disappointments and tragedies, they can become disappointed and bitter. But when mended by a hand of infinite patience and love, the finished product will be a work of exquisite beauty and effectiveness; a life which could only reach its wholeness after it was broken.

If you feel broken, remember that you are a work of art! And you may not actually be complete until the pieces are reassembled and bonded with a golden filigree of love.

Personal and Professional Growth through Loss

One of my colleagues, a rabbi we'll call Mark, made one of his life's most important, and fulfilling breakthroughs as a result of one of his most disappointing losses. Ten years ago, he had just turned fifty and had been the rabbi at his latest synagogue for nine years.

"The incoming president had been talking to me about giving me tenure. It used to be the case in the rabbinate that after a rabbi served nine or ten years at one synagogue, he'd be given this security, a lifetime tenure," Mark recalls. "I should've seen the handwriting on the wall, but I didn't.

Quite to my surprise, I lost my job. I was told not just that I wasn't being given a life tenure, but that I was being let go. The outgoing and incoming presidents wanted to give me tenure, but others didn't want me to stay."

Mark was in shock; angry, grieving, and afraid that the future might not hold much for him. "I wish I had a nickel for everyone who said to me when the ax fell, 'When God closes a door, he opens a window.' A person doesn't want to hear that when he's grieving. You know there will be some kind of future, but in the meantime you have to deal with this loss. I found that it's not so easy for a fifty-year-old to get another position," he remembers. "I thought that maybe I should retrain myself and get into something where my age wouldn't be held against me. Even though I'd never envisioned myself a counselor, only a rabbi, I decided to take some classes in counseling, and as luck would have it, that year I wasn't offered anything of consequence as a rabbi, so I took that year off and took courses."

Mark realized that he had a lot of talent and skills in this area, and he also made other important discoveries. "Not only did taking these courses give me new skills, they also made me a better rabbi. And the counseling helped me deal with my own grief," he says. "I got a position as a part-time rabbi at a synagogue and worked there while I studied at a nearby college. The more courses I took, the more I realized not only how much more there was for me to learn as a rabbi, but that my true calling was to be a pastoral counselor, a chaplain, instead of a pulpit rabbi. So I studied to become a chaplain."

Mark eventually became the rabbi at a Jewish nursing facility, and got his Doctor of Ministry degree. "I honestly believe that if I were to go back to the pulpit now, I'd be a much better pulpit rabbi. I have much better skills because of my studies as a counselor and a chaplain. When I was still studying counseling and working part-time as a pulpit rabbi, I remember I gave a sermon, and when I finished, there wasn't a sound to be heard. The silence was broken when a woman somewhere in the congregation said, 'Beautiful.' That moment showed me that I'd been able to make an impact, that what I'd learned studying to be a counselor had made a difference," Mark says. "Many years ago, when I was studying to be a rabbi, they didn't teach this to us. They're just starting to offer counseling education in rabbinical schools."

Mark's biggest professional loss ended up leading to his biggest professional success, and his biggest personal fulfillment. His wife, who had grieved with him, also grew because of his loss. She had been a working professional and went back to school to get her doctorate, too. "I was never as happy as a pulpit rabbi as I am as a chaplain," Mark says. "There is plenty of opportunity, plenty of growth to come, but I didn't want to hear it when I was going through it. I see it now. Since I had to do it, I made the best of it. Looking back, I see that not getting tenure and not getting my contract renewed was the best thing that could've happened."

Embracing Growth

People often put a value on loss, and they shouldn't. They say, "This loss was bad, that loss was good." Loss isn't bad or good, it just is. It's loss. It's neutral. So don't feel guilty when you think your life will be okay—or better—after what you consider a major loss. Don't resist the growth that comes after loss. You have nothing to feel guilty about.

Don't resist recovering from grief because you feel guilty about feeling better, especially if your loss is the death of a loved one. Remember that Psalm 66 shows us that loss, and our healing, "refines" us, and from those experiences we can't help but grow.

CHAPTER 13

Legacy

The Story: Moses's Legacy, from the Book of Deuteronomy

⌒

ALL OF US want to leave a legacy, especially those who are pondering death. A legacy is someone's way of saying, "I don't want to be forgotten; I want to be remembered for something I contributed." You will find not just knowledge but comfort, inspiration, wisdom, and healing in remembering what you've learned from those who have died, and from carrying on their legacy.

In Deuteronomy, Moses presented God's laws to the Israelites and then said in Deuteronomy 32:46–47, "Set your heart unto all the words wherewith I testify against you this day; that ye may charge your children therewith to observe to do all the words of this law. For it is no vain thing for you; because it is your life, and through this thing ye shall prolong your days upon the land, whither ye go over the Jordan to possess it." Moses didn't enter Israel—the Promised Land— with the Israelites, but he taught them all he could, leaving them a legacy, before he went up to Mt. Nebo to die.

We have all been to funerals where friends and relatives tell stories about the person who has died. When I meet with the family the day before the funeral, I invite them to choose two or three representatives who will share their reminiscences with those present at the service. These stories are the answers to the questions: *Who exactly was this person? What were their passions? What values moved them to action? What contributions did they make to the world? How did they leave it better than they found it?* After these sometimes tearful—and sometimes humorous, which is also appropriate—funeral tributes, I then say: "If you want to know how to truly mourn this person, if you want to keep them alive and present in your hearts even after they have left this world, you need to embrace what was important to them, for these were their gifts to us, this was their legacy."

There are two kinds of legacies: tangible and intangible. A tangible legacy is the person's work or creations, the product of their work, the history they documented, and the like. An intangible legacy is the person's values, the memories you have of the person, and how that person touched and changed the world (from their home and neighborhood to the whole world) and the people in it (from those they knew to people they never even met). An intangible legacy can turn into a tangible one when you inspire someone and that person goes on to do or create something that carries on your legacy, as well as, ultimately, their own.

A person's legacy lives on as long as there are people to carry it on. We keep people's legacies alive in ways we might not even realize: by displaying photos, telling stories, talking about them, sharing their wisdom, having something they owned, and passing their possessions and wisdom on to the next generation. When you share your late loved one's legacy, it keeps their spirit and contributions (and I don't mean financial) alive in your heart, in others' hearts, and out in the world.

Legacies in Action

Storytelling, the sharing of wisdom, is perhaps the oldest form of legacy. It's the passing on of part of a person's history, and keeping that history alive to benefit all who hear it.

A woman we'll call Lee loves to pass along tidbits of wisdom from family, friends, and colleagues who have died. These are little stories or one-liners that she's always remembered, that have helped her, amused her, or given her food for thought. You don't have to be Moses to have valuable wisdom and ideas to pass along.

"Sharing their words not only helps people, including plenty of folks they didn't even know, but it also keeps their memories very much alive, not just for me, but for others," says Lee. "Their wisdom, their humor lives on, long after they're dead, and I think that is great. Some of them have been gone for decades, or even a hundred years, but their impact is still felt today. You don't have to be famous for your words to live on long after you do." Although, when your words *do* live on long after you do, that does kind of make you famous, doesn't it?

When we're grieving, sharing someone's legacy can be a powerful healing tool. Here are two legacy stories, the first about a young man who died at the age of thirty-four, the other about an older man who is still going strong at the age of ninety. The first, Jonathan Schwartz, had no idea that he was leaving a legacy; the second, Tom Breslauer, is still creating his.

Jonathan Schwartz's Legacy in Words and Music

When Betty Barsha Hedenberg's only child, her son, Jonathan Schwartz, died in 2002 at only thirty-four, she began her healing process by making sure that Jonathan's considerable creative talent did not die with him. "Jonathan was a gift from God," Betty says. "He was beautiful, intelligent, sensitive, a helper. He was a gifted musician, artist, and poet."

At five, Jonathan had surgery to repair a congenital heart defect. Betty divorced when Jonathan was twelve, and she became a single, professional working mother. When Jonathan was fifteen, he was diagnosed with schizophrenia. Already a promising French horn player, he continued with his schooling and the music he loved while he battled his illness. While still in high school, he played in the youth orchestra at the California Institute of the Arts and with an ensemble at the University of Southern California. At eighteen, he made his debut with the West Valley Chamber Orchestra. After graduating from high school in 1986, he studied with the Los Angeles Philharmonic's principal horn, and at the prestigious Aspen Music Festival for the first of five summers.

Jonathan went to New York City and attended Julliard on full scholarship. In his third year there he was hospital-ized for psychiatric treatment a number of times and wasn't well enough to complete his studies and graduate. He rallied, and in the fall of 1989 he went to Israel to play for a season with the Jerusalem Symphony as principal horn. He did very well with the symphony and saw a psy-chiatrist in Jerusalem who monitored his medication.

While in Jerusalem, he fell in love with Agnes, a Hun-garian musician he'd first met in Aspen, who was now playing the viola for a season with the symphony. Jonathan and Agnes came back to the United States in the summer of 1990 and studied again at the Aspen Music Festival. They married there, and in the fall moved to Arizona, where Jonathan began playing with the Phoenix Sym-phony. Jonathan began spiraling downward again late that fall. In January 1991 their son, Christopher, was born. A few months later, Jonathan was no longer stable enough to work, and the Phoenix Symphony had to let him go. They moved from Phoenix to Los Angeles and lived with Jonathan's mother, Betty, for a few months before getting their own place.

Betty had always given Jonathan her complete support. Her frustrations at the illness that was robbing her talented son of a normal life were not aimed at Jonathan; they were aimed at God. "Was I angry? Oh, probably," she recalls. "I thought, 'Oh, God, why did you do this?' I was looking for reasons, but there are no reasons, it's random. There's sup-posed to be a genetic component to schizophrenia.

Jonathan's father's sister was probably schizophrenic, but I don't know if she was diagnosed. I never met her. Jonathan's father's mother was also not quite right."

Jonathan could no longer perform as a musician. His illness was too unstable. He'd always written poetry, but now he began to write more and to read his poems to his mother.

In August 1992, when Christopher was about eighteen months old, Jonathan and Agnes went to Hungary to visit her family, who hadn't yet seen their grandson. The visit became a move, and they gave up their California apartment and stayed with Agnes's parents for four months. Then they moved to Germany, where Agnes found a job performing with an orchestra. Jonathan still wasn't well enough to perform. Six months later, in June 1993, Agnes sent Jonathan back to California, because he was so unstable that it was no longer safe for him to be around his two-and-a-half-year-old son. The couple didn't divorce, but they would never live together, or see each other, again.

Betty picked up Jonathan at the airport, they went out to eat, and then she took him directly to the hospital, where he stayed for two weeks. After his release, he went to live at a group home. He was only twenty-five, and his brilliant but short-lived musical career was over. He was on disability. He turned his creative attentions to his poetry.

In 1998 Jonathan moved to New York City. "Jonathan always knew when he needed to go to the hospital, and he'd take himself there, and he never refused to take his medication," Betty recalls. "Both are very unusual for a schizophrenic." When his plane landed in New York,

Jonathan went directly to the hospital. After his release, he moved into an apartment that had psychiatric supervision. For the next four years he lived in New York and wrote poetry. Agnes remained in Germany and was no longer in contact with Jonathan, but she kept in touch with Betty.

Betty often visited Jonathan in New York and was planning to fly there on December 28, 2002, to stay a week at a cousin's house and see Jonathan every day. "On Christmas Eve, he called," Betty remembers. "He'd gotten some nice gifts at the treatment center where he lived. He asked me what I was doing, and I told him I'd been looking at a recipe called Death by Chocolate Cookie. He asked if I'd make it sometime, and I said absolutely."

When Jonathan had surgery at five to fix a congenital heart defect, the doctors had put a Teflon patch on it, saying that it would hold and that his prognosis was excellent. But the schizophrenia medication caused him to put on weight, and he became diabetic. The physician at the treatment center where he lived was a cardiologist, and she had him on heart medication and monitored him. The Teflon was holding up, but he was very overweight, so the rate at which his heart pumped blood out was too low.

"Our conversation ended with 'I love you, Mom,' and 'I love you, too, Jonathan. I'll call you tomorrow morning to wish you a Merry Christmas.' We hung up," Betty remembers. "That was the last conversation we had. We think he had a ventricular fibrillation and he died over night in his sleep."

When Betty went to identify her son's body at the morgue, she said, "I've come to take you home." Betty had him cremated, and she keeps his ashes at her home. "On the urn, I have a plate that says: 'Jonathan, principal horn,' and the date of his birth and his death. Every day I talk to him, I touch the urn. It is comforting to have him with me."

When Betty went through Jonathan's poetry notebooks, she discovered the vast amount of poetry he'd been writing all those years, some of which he'd read to her. "I went through the poetry, and the pages were torn, blotted, stained, and creased. I had to put the pages back together," she remembers. "What meant the most to me was being able to pull all of his poetry together."

She published *From the Dark Side: The Collected Poetry of Jonathan Schwartz* (Santa Clarita, CA: Jonathan Books, 2005), which includes a preface in which she tells Jonathan's life story, and she collected recordings of his French horn performances and made a CD. "It would've been a deeper tragedy to allow his work to slip into oblivion," she says. "I cry when I listen to his music and read his poetry, but crying doesn't make you weak. You have to vent. Doing the poetry book and the CD strengthened me."

She had only one hundred copies of *From the Dark Side* printed and never thought there might be interest beyond family, friends, and Jonathan's colleagues. She could not have been more wrong. On a lark, she submitted the book in the poetry category of the prestigious Independent Publisher Book Awards (IPPY Awards). *From the Dark Side* won the 2006 IPPY Award for best poetry book, beating competition that included a host of established, honored poets.

Betty has since created the publishing imprint Jonathan Books, and *From the Dark Side* is in its second printing. Betty is promoting and distributing her son's legacy nationwide. Betty also established the Jonathan M. Schwartz Memorial Scholarship, for students of the French horn, at Julliard. When Betty dies, the scholarship will be permanently funded from her trust. When the book came out, a friend said to Betty, "This is twice you've given life to Jonathan."

A legacy is a rebirth. It is indeed a "second life," another opportunity for others to embrace your values, to live out your life dreams, just as you did. And who knows whether your own legacy might be a continuation of theirs? What better legacy could there ever be?

Sharing her son's legacy has been crucial to Betty's grief recovery process. When we suffer a loss, we often feel powerless. But a legacy, no matter what form it takes, removes that sense of powerlessness and helps us turn our loss into a gift to the world. Jonathan Schwartz loved himself enough to take care of himself, and he loved the rest of humanity enough to show it through his music and his poetry.

Betty Barsha Hedenberg says her son was "the most beautiful thing that ever happened to me." Now, by sharing his legacy, she can share her blessing with the rest of us.

> *Is there no one like me?*
> *To share my grief, and to share my joy?*

—*From "Question," by Jonathan Schwartz*

Coming to America from Dachau with Five Dollars in His Pocket

Tom Breslauer is a Holocaust survivor, former businessman, long-time community volunteer, and New York University graduate (class of 1989, at age seventy-one!). Now ninety years old, Tom has a new passion: speaking to students in and around his hometown of Stroudsburg, Pennsylvania, about his experiences. His story has also been documented by Holocaust survivors who participate in Steven Spielberg's Shoah Visual History Foundations project, which videotapes eyewitness Holocaust survivor testimony all over the world.

Tom remembers the Germany of his boyhood as a kind of paradise. He grew up in Hamburg, playing soccer under the elevated train, tinkering with his crystal radio set, and hiking and biking with the Boy Scouts, unaware that as Jews he and his family were somehow different. "Society was completely integrated," he recalled. Tom and his sister, Ilse, were raised by a "warm, loving mother who worked all the time" and took in borders to keep the family together. His father was killed in the Battle of the Somme six months before Tom was born. His mother never remarried. In many ways, "I was to my mother the man she never had," Tom said.

He also remembers November 9, 1938, as clearly as if it were yesterday. At the time, Tom was working in his uncle's shoe factory in Offenbach, being groomed to take over the enterprise. On that day, he and forty other Jewish neighbors were rounded up by two silent SS men. A few days later they boarded trains to be transported to Dachau. There, in Barracks 10, room 28, still dressed in the clothes he had been wearing on his arrest, Tom began four months of incarceration, one among thousands of Jews, repeat criminals, gypsies, and Seventh Day Adventists. Forced marching and calisthenics were part of the daily routine. "I tried to stay in the middle of a formation, do the pushups, march, whatever we were ordered to do." He worried constantly about what might have happened to his mother and sister.

The rise of the Nazis had caught everyone by surprise. "Between 1926 and 1933 there were six or seven elections," Tom recalled. "There were twenty-five political parties and people were used to many changes in the government. We really didn't believe [Hitler] would last." As the Nazi party took control, "everything changed. People were suddenly afraid to recognize their Jewish neighbors. My family had lived here more than two hundred years. I considered myself German who happened to have a Jewish religion." Despite these changes, his mother insisted she would be all right: "Your father died for the fatherland," she insisted, "don't worry about me."

In March of 1939 Tom was released from Dachau and, thanks to his mother's having secured the necessary papers, was able to emigrate to the United States. He never saw her again.

Tom Breslauer lived the dream of emigrants to America.

He started out with a job in a shoe factory on 14th Street in New York City, living in one room at 137th Street and Riverside Drive. He attended George Washington High School to improve his English. While in New York, he met Lisle Wolfrom, also an emigrant from Germany—"It was love at first sight"—married her, and eventually moved to Stroudsburg, where he would go on to found his own, very successful women's wear manufacturing company named for his wife. The Breslauers raised their two sons in Stroudsburg and were active in the community. Tom became the president of the synagogue. In 1983 he sold his business and enrolled at New York University, graduating in 1989 with a bachelor's degree in humanities.

That same year, Tom, by then a successful American businessman and pillar of his community, was invited to return to Hamburg for the first time since he left, to learn what had happened to his mother. He discovered that she had been arrested in December 1941 and sent to a farm. Because she had a heart condition and could not do the work, she was executed at the age of fifty-two, one of six thousand Jews of Hamburg who were killed, including his grandparents and an uncle.

Tom was overwhelmed when he found out what had happened to his mother. He fell into a deep depression. "When I returned from Germany, I went to see a psychologist friend of mine. He told me that the best way for me to deal with the feelings I was having was to pretend my mother's death just happened. So for seven days I said Kaddish for my mother. I went to synagogue and prayed for her. I treated her death as a fresh wound. And this healed me. I was finally able to talk to my children about my experiences."

And he talked to everyone else's children as well. Tom had decided that he would do all he could to teach the next generation about the evils of hatred and the rewards of respect. He was joined in this vision by his new wife, Camille Bianco, whom he met when they were both active in the local arts council. He asked Camille to marry him in 1992 while on a plane to visit his sister in England—"I asked her then so she couldn't back out!"

Together they travel all over the Northeast, visiting classroom after classroom, from elementary school to high school to college. He tells his story with a gentle passion that never fails him. Tom has embraced this new career for himself—I believe he is on act 4 or 5 in his ninety-year-old life, and he loves it! He is a living witness to the Holocaust to his young students. He is in demand as a lecturer and has received more than two thousand letters of appreciation from schoolchildren and adults. "The inspiring light of your life will live in our hearts forever," writes a fan. "Your age never mattered to the minds of my students," writes another, "your age dazzled them, they listened with intense reverence and respect, awed by your every word."

It might have been normal for Tom to be angry about what the Nazis had done to him and his family, but that was not his way. No, my friend Tom preferred to face forward, not backward, and he is a beacon to all of those who are fortunate enough to hear him speak. Tom exudes hope. He could have given up, as so many other Holocaust survivors have done—and who would blame him? But he has chosen instead to become a treasured elder of this world, one of our modern-day wise men who has chosen to bequeath his wisdom to others so that evil can one day be defeated.

Tom's legacy is to teach the next generation that we all must live in this world together; that we do not have to love everyone but that we do have to respect everyone. Tom has lost so much—his first wife, family, homeland, and community. His past was snatched from him at an early age. But he never gave up, and we are the fortunate beneficiaries.

> I try and teach people what it is like to become a non-person; to be invisible to those around you. It is such a lonely place and I want people to know what it is like So they can prevent it from happening to those around them.
>
> Yes, it is difficult for me. But unless I tell you, how would you know?
> Teaching tolerance is what I do.
> —Tom Breslauer

Moses never got to reach the Promised Land, but he did get to look at it from the top of Mt. Nebo. It wasn't all that he wanted, but it was enough. He knew there would be others to follow in his footsteps, and that was sufficient. He was at peace, for he knew his legacy would live on. And it did. We should all be as lucky.

Chapter 14

The Future: Creating New Relationships and Creating a New Family

The Story: Lessons from the Book of Ruth

IF YOUR GRIEF recovery journey has come this far, your wandering is almost over and, like Moses, you have reached the mountaintop overlooking your Promised Land. You may remember when you began, how perilous and insurmountable the journey had seemed, from the time you received the news that your loved one had died. You have done well, and you are now ready to create your future.

The book of Ruth tells us that when Ruth's husband died, she stayed in Moab with her widowed mother-in-law, Naomi. Then, although Ruth was a Moabite, she went with Naomi to Bethlehem, where Naomi had been born and raised. In Ruth 1:16–17, Ruth said to Naomi, "Do not entreat me to leave you, to turn back from you. For wherever you will go, there I will go; wherever you will lodge, I will lodge; your people shall be my people, and your God my God; wherever you will die, I will die, and there I will be buried. Only death will separate us." The two women thus preserved and strengthened their family bond. In Bethlehem, Ruth then continued the creation of her new family by marrying Boaz and having a son, Obed. Out of this new family, greatness came: Obed's grandson was King David.

After a loss of any kind, by any means, you can create a new future, and that includes new opportunities, circumstances, relationships, and even a new family.

Creating New Relationships

It is always a bad idea to go into a new relationship when you are on the rebound, and when you haven't healed from your loss. When you're wounded and trying to avoid being alone, you want someone to take the place of the beloved you lost. But rather than seeing this new person for who he or she is, this new object of your attention is merely a substitute for the loved one you lost. You didn't stop having a lot of love to give just because you lost your loved one, and you want someone to receive this love, so you connect with someone on the rebound, or out of emotional pain. You're used to being part of a couple, and it feels strange not to be. You think you'll resolve all of these uncomfortable feelings simply by entering into a relationship with someone just to fill the void.

People do this all the time, and they usually choose their mirror image: *My pain falls in love with your pain.* You fall for someone who's also suffering some kind of loss and hasn't healed. You bond on your grieving and on both of your attempts to fill a void. If you haven't healed, you could have one relationship after another on the rebound for years. Or you could have your first relationship five years after the loss and that would be considered a rebound relationship. Rebound is more about your emotional state than about time.

This kind of relationship is not based on anything real or healthy. It is based on negative aspects, not positive ones. It's based on fear, loneliness, and pain, rather than love, passion, respect, and compatibility. You find yourself comparing this new person to the one you lost. And if the two of you try to create a new family, you're likely to find yourself constantly comparing it to the "old" one. None of this is healthy or fair. These relationships don't turn out well. They often end, or if they continue, they continue miserably.

So how do you do it right? When will you be ready for love again? When you've gone through your grief and recovered from it. And that takes time. Your healing may come sooner or later than someone else's, so don't compare yourself to others.

How will you know you're ready? You'll be able to feel it, and know the difference between moving on in a healthy way and starting a new relationship and being on the rebound and starting one while you're still in a lot of pain, where you know deep down that you're just trying to fill a void and avoid being alone.

You've probably been on the rebound before. Who among us hasn't? And you know what that feels like, even when you try to tell yourself that you're not on the rebound. It's a pretty thin layer of denial—you don't have to dig too deep to get to the truth because it's right there under the surface. So you'll also know when you're not on the rebound. You will know you have healed when the mention of your lost beloved's name doesn't cause an ache in your heart, in your gut. As long as it does, you haven't healed.

We know when we've physically healed, because it's usually pretty obvious. But figuring out when we've emotionally healed can be tricky sometimes because of the lies we tell ourselves so that we don't have to be alone. Your broken leg doesn't lie, but your broken heart will. You know that your heart hasn't healed yet, but your heart is in so much pain, and it wants to stop that pain, so it tells you that the pain will stop if you focus on someone new. This is the lie that your heart tells you.

Feeling good about someone else is wonderful, but it won't heal your broken heart. It can contribute to the healing if your relationship with the new person is healthy, but without all of the other aspects of what it takes to heal, you won't heal. The new relationship is not a magic bullet, a miracle cure.

Loving someone else is a very small part of the healing equation. It is a very nice Band-Aid on the boo-boo, but it's still just a Band-Aid. You still have to heal the wound under it. If you put a Band-Aid on a wound that hasn't been cleaned and disinfected, it can get infected under that nice Band-Aid. The cleaning and disinfecting in this analogy is the grief recovery process, including dealing with all of the issues you've read about in this book, emotionally completing the lost relationship, and finally letting go of it.

A broken relationship, or the death of your beloved, feels like an amputation. You feel like you've lost a limb, but you can still feel the limb's presence in a way, and you can sense pain in that limb, even though it's not there. In medicine, that is called the phantom effect. You still feel a phantom pain in the limb, as if it were still there.

When you lose a loved one who was part of you, it feels like part of you is missing. And that makes sense. In a very real way, part of you *is* missing. But you must allow that wound to heal before you attach a new part to you, a new person to you.

Creating a New Family

The biggest challenge to creating a new family is understanding that this is, literally, a new family. It is not the old family, or even a variation of the old family. It is a fresh beginning. Everyone involved is now a member of the new family. Do not see this situation as old family members integrating with new family members, because that is a prescription for complications, as the question of who is supposed to fit in with whom arises. Are the old family members supposed to adapt to the new ones, or are the new ones supposed to adapt to the old ones?

Instead, keep in mind that this situation is a brand-new family for everyone. No one is labeled "old" or "new," so no one is expected to take a role in a power play. These are not old team members coming together with new team members. This is a brand-new team. This is a new family unit that shouldn't be pressured into conforming to the old family unit, and its new members shouldn't be pressured to do that, either. Everyone starts with a clean slate, so that all the members come together to create something brand-new.

Before you can successfully create a new family, you must grieve the old family setup. You can't expect the new spouse to be a carbon copy of the previous one and do everything the same way. A new family can only succeed when there are no power games, no resentment, no competition, no comparisons, and no judging. This is especially important when dealing with children who resent the presence of stepparents, either after a divorce or the death of a parent.

The Rabinowitz Bunch

While the story of Naomi, Ruth, and Boaz gives us hope, a modern-day family in Pennsylvania takes that hope to great heights. Norman and Marcie Rabinowitz are an extreme version of creating a future, creating new relationships, and creating a new family—a testament to how open your heart can be after loss. I'm sure you've all heard the expression, "You have to kiss a lot of frogs before you find your prince." It refers, of course, to the fairytale in which the young maiden kisses a frog and it turns into a prince. And, of course, they live happily ever after. Frogs brought Norm and Marcie together, and, lucky Marcie, she got the prince without ever having to lock lips with even one frog.

In 1983 Norman was a divorced father with a young son, and Marcie was a divorced mother with two young daughters. "Both of us were single custodial parents, and we both belonged to Parents without Partners," Norm recalls. "We met at an event called Night of the Frogs, and we were listening to the bullfrogs' mating calls. Marcie's daughters were scared of the frogs' noises, and that is how we met. I was trying to console and quell the fears of two little girls. Marcie and I started dating soon after that."

Two years later, they got married. They wanted to add to their new family but ran into difficulties, so they tried fertility treatments. When those didn't work, Marcie and Norm began applying to adopt, and in the meantime decided to be foster parents. They didn't plan to take the idea as far as it ended up going. "It evolved, and each child was brought into the family based on what they needed and what we needed," Marcie says. "Each child touched our hearts, and we hope we've made a difference in their lives." Marcie and Norm estimate that they have fostered about two hundred children in the last twenty years.

But that is not all. Along the way, they also adopted six kids, five of whom had first been their foster children. "We knew that this is what we wanted to do, that we were doing something good for them and for our family," says Norm. "We couldn't let them go back to where they came from." Their children are white, black, multiracial, multicultural, and Hispanic. And now all of them are also Jewish.

Today Norm and Marcie pass along their considerable experience, not only as adoptive parents, but also as veterans of the often challenging bureaucratic road to adoption. They counsel adoptive and foster parents, especially on transracial adoption, and speak frequently at conferences.

When Marcie and her two daughters created a new family with Norm and his son, they had no idea that their family would continue to evolve, but it did, and they became "new" over and over again, ultimately including a total of nine children. Marcie beams proudly: "All of the kids adamantly believe that they are a family."

My Final Thoughts

When Ruth said to Naomi, "Wherever you will go, there I will go," she spoke *to* us, and *for* us as well. The word "wherever" contains within it a question *and* an answer. The question is "Where?" And in the end, that is as good a question about grief as I know. For when loss comes into our lives, we have no idea where our journey will take us, over what hills and valleys we will traverse, what truths we will discover about ourselves along the way, or how it all will end. The answer to the question "Where?" is "Wherever," which means we are not to know our destination at the beginning of the trip. While it is the mystery of the "where" that frightens us, it is the discovery of the "wherever" that challenges and encourages us.

Perhaps it makes perfect sense for the question and the answer to be intertwined in the same word, for as you come to the end this book, you now know the truth—that your "where" will in time lead you to your "wherever."

Loss *will* lead you to discovery, pain will lead to joy, mourning will lead to morning. And then you will be healed.

May your "where" and your "wherever" both bring you peace. And God created hope . . . forever!

Epilogue

⁓

WHILE I WAS writing *And God Created Hope,* I moved to Stroudsburg, Pennsylvania, to become Rabbi at Temple Israel of the Poconos. As part of the move, I needed to find new doctors, so I made an appointment with one of the local specialists. He suggested that I have my lungs checked as part of a thorough physical exam.

He scheduled me for a CAT scan, expecting to find nothing out of the ordinary. Well, surprise, surprise! When I returned to the doctor for the results, he told me there was a spot on my lung, and he could not rule out lung cancer.

Next, he scheduled me to have a PET scan, which would show if anything was going on in my throat. Three days later I went to the surgery center, and through an IV, they inserted some dye, which flowed through my entire upper body so I could be scanned. I lay still for sixty-five minutes, trying to "zone out," actually counting the seconds (one thousand one, one thousand two, one thousand three . . .) and trying to act like the macho man that I did not feel like.

My doctor had scheduled the next appointment for a week later. I asked him for an earlier date, but he said it would take that long for the results and the evaluation of the scan. It turned out that the results and evaluation were completed two hours after the test, but I didn't know that then. So I had a whole week to think about the possibility that I might be dying of lung cancer. What made it really scary was that my mother had died of lung cancer. She was a heavy smoker. I've never smoked, but I had already pre- sumed that this might be genetic and that my life was over. And so I began to plan.

What would I do with the time I had left? First, would I take chemo and radiation for the cancer? I decided absolutely not, since I didn't want to spend the next year suffering through mind-and-body-torturing treatments that would, at best, give me maybe another month or two of life, life that wasn't really life at all. I've seen too many of my congregants and friends go through that, and I knew it was not for me.

Would I quit my job as rabbi? Yes, I would do that imme- diately upon receiving the test results and cancer diagnosis, and I even began working on my final sermon. I would tell my new congregation that there are places in this world that I want to visit with my wife, Ellen, and that I especially need to return to Israel for a final visit, so I'd be resigning from the pulpit. I would thank my congregants for the les- sons they had already taught me even in the short time we had together, and I would ask their forgiveness for any pain

I had caused them. I would complete my relationship with them before I left.

After seeing other parts of the world, I would return home and begin to travel all across the country, giving a lecture to anyone who might be interested titled "Final Life Thoughts of a Grateful Rabbi." During the lecture, I would talk about how gratitude was the first feeling I'd had after learning of my impending death. Above all, I would say I'm grateful for the life I've been granted, and I consider my life a precious gift to me from God. After gratitude would come everything else, all my other feelings and thoughts. I would talk about how the world can be repaired only when gratitude replaces entitlement, when we move outside ourselves toward others in our lives.

When I thought about dying, I realized that I wasn't angry. I was just sad that I wouldn't live to see my kids' life-cycle events or share in the lives of my grandchildren. I felt like my hopes, dreams, and aspirations had been reached, and that I would die happy and fulfilled. If my time had come, I would be ready, unafraid, and pleased with what I'd accomplished in my life. I knew that I had mattered to a lot of folks, and my teachings and memories would be my final gift to them and to the universe.

I believe that when our mission on this earth is accomplished, we can be ready and prepared to leave the world for whatever comes next. The problem is, *Who among us knows when their missions have been accomplished?* We don't. So if God has decided that my earthly purpose has been fulfilled, who am I to argue?

I've known too many people who have lived "too long." They spent their final years in pain or totally unable to communicate with those they loved. I would, indeed, be fortunate, because I would leave this life on my own terms, proud and grateful. Smart guy that I am, I was sure I had it all figured out.

Needless to say, thank God, the results came back showing that the spot on my lung was some benign scar tissue left over from who-knows-what and who-knows-when. I was elated. I really was. But to tell the deep, dark, honest-to-God truth, I was just a wee bit disappointed at the same time. I was actually looking forward to the last year of my life. I was going to be able to fill the closing chapter of my existence with passion! Between seeing the world, teaching people across the country the truths I'd learned, and finishing this book on grief and hope, my days would be filled with joy and creativity. They would be filled with life, not death, and when the end came, I would feel that my life had been well worth my fifty-nine years of effort.

That is my story, and it has a happy ending.

Sort of.

The gnawing-in-my-gut question I continue to ask myself ever since this happened is: *What's stopping me from doing all those things I was going to do if I was going to die?* How many of them can I still do right now, even without a death sentence hanging over me? Why do I have to wait until the angel of death comes calling for me, *for real?*

These are *the real questions,* not thoughts of dying one day, that continue to haunt me.

Acknowledgments

I **CREATED THIS** book from the knowledge and experiences I have gathered from many sources, including those who have taught me, both personally and professionally.

Bubbe B., my grandmother, taught me how to be a Jew; my parents, Rose and Abe Glazer, of blessed memory, first set me on the path to my life's work; and my sister, Gail, and my brother, Jerry, have often illuminated that path.

Rabbi Harry H. Epstein, of blessed memory, was my rabbinic "father," took me under his wing when I was only a child, sponsored my education, and taught me how to be a mensch.

Amanda P. Ayo was my childhood piano teacher. She wanted me to be a symphony conductor, but I ended up a rabbi. She died before I could tell her that her instincts had been correct. I *did* grow up to do what she had envisioned, but with a twist. I am a conductor, but not of a group of musicians. The "symphony" I conduct is all of God's children, and I see the image of each one playing their own "instrument": their own life.

Rabbi Kenny Berger, of blessed memory, was my best friend then and now. We grew up together. He taught me how to be a rabbi, how to laugh at myself, and how to love myself. He taught all of us how not to have "if onlys."

I'd like to thank Nina. L. Diamond, my editor and literary mind reader, who "gets" me and has been able to "read between my lines."

My agent, Mollie Glick of the Jean V. Naggar Literary Agency, understood immediately what I was trying to accomplish and found me just the right publishing home.

From the first conversation we had, my publisher and editor, Matthew Lore, has been supportive and thorough and has shared my desire to have my thoughts heard by those who are grieving. His former assistant, Peter Jacoby, was a great help throughout the initial stages of the publishing process.

Patricia L. Lee has been a delight to work with as she expertly turned the manuscript into a computer disk.

Thank-you to Russell Friedman, executive director of the Grief Recovery Institute, for his gracious foreword. Russell and his *Grief Recovery Handbook* coauthor, institute founder John James, taught me how to help myself and others heal.

Thank-you to Carol O'Neill, my editor at the *Pocono Record,* which publishes my monthly column, "Your Grief Matters."

Rabbi Edwin Friedman, of blessed memory, taught me how to be a leader; Rabbi David Mogilner, of blessed memory, taught me that being a rabbi is just like being a camp counselor; Rabbi Jack Bloom taught me everything I know about being a "symbolic exemplar" and an accessible, joyous role model; Dr. Randy Nichols, head of the Doctor of Ministry program at Princeton Theological Seminary, trained me to be a scholar; Maria Trozzi, author of *Talking with Children about Loss* (New York: Perigee, 1999), taught me how to approach grief; Paula Klein first pointed me in the direction of grief education and counseling; and my business coach, Lynn McIntyre Coffey, taught me how to put everything all together.

Thank-you to the members of my congregation, Temple Israel of the Poconos, who have encouraged me to pursue my passion in writing this book, and to my colleagues in the Rabbinical Assembly, who have always been a source of inspiration.

This book would not have been possible without the continued support of Ruth Ann Hornisch; Abe Novogrodsky; Harriett Fox; Debbie Betz; Linda Georgian; Don and Sheila Goldstein; Dr. Yale Samole; Leon Steinberg, of blessed memory; Joe Zelman, of blessed memory, and my longtime friend Bruin Lipman.

Thank you to my children, Rafi, Shoshi, Ilan, and Avi, and to their mother, Donna.

My wife, Ellen Mossman Glazer, has given me hope in the midst of loss, has taught me that we're all entitled to be happy, and has shown me how.

Finally, my gratitude to all of the people who have shared their stories with me, and now, with you, the readers of *And God Created Hope.*

Rabbi Mel Glazer would be pleased to hear your reactions to *And God Created Hope*. Call him at 877-LECHAIM (ToLife!).